It's a Journey.... St

Glenda Clarke

Everyone has a Journey Path

It's A Journey......Step by Step
Special dedication and in Loving memory to my Angel. My first niece Angelica. (My Gala Gee) who was my cheerleader and Pusher in so many ways. You gave and showed me so much love. I thank you for encouraging me to write this book. I miss you so much and wish you was here to this major accomplishment. I can say Hallelujah! I did this baby girl! (tears) You meant so much to me and you will forever be treasured in my heart.
Loving you Always, Your Aunt Glenda

Words of Acknowledgements

I would first like to thank My Lord and Savior Jesus Christ for allowing me to go through this journey process, for it had not been for him; there would not be a me. I fought so long and burned the midnight oil to for fill one of my dreams and that was to write this book and allow others to know that they are not alone and that there is a time, season and reason for everything. Thank you to the many that don't and didn't see me as good enough. When man says No God says Yes!

To my beautiful and amazing children, you are all my presents from God, and I thank God for each one of you. You have brought so much joy to my life and can go on and on about each one of you. Daily I've watched you grow, mature and became beautiful young women and an awesome Man. Let no one mistreat you, know your worth and know I've taught you that you are all important and have voices; continue to go the path that God wants you to go not what Mommy, Daddy or anyone else wants or tells you. Keep God first and he will be with you acknowledge him he will direct your path. I am truly blessed to be alive if it had not been for God, prayers and my Children's grandmother not an ex-mother-in-law because of who she is in my life, she's not ex out of my life. she's still a mother to me even today. We may have bumped heads from time to time, but I give honor where it's due. Mom was there with and for me every step of the way and set the example to myself and to my kids as a grandmother and their kids today, even when my own immediate family was not there for me at times. God thank you for allowing me to be alive to say again and see my grandchildren all 5 of their births, and to be honored to have cut all their umbilical cords. What an honor and privilege. To my Bestie James; Thank you so much for showing me nothing but love and sharing your heart years ago also filled with memories and laughter that people take for granted today, again I say to you thank you. To my Eldest Sister Viv who said: I can't wait to read it and go for it! that I can do all things through Christ. My Youngest Sister Teisha who said I encourage you to finish this and I want to read it first and support you anyway I can to get this out and make this happen with you. Also, for saying you are proud of me!! (Tears) SFL (one of a kind) Vanessa Blue-Swann that was for me in the beginning from day one, both unsaved with our young craziness (Laughing) marriage, children, saved, laughter and fun tears, pain, divorces, elevating in Christ, remarriage,   My God I can go on (smiling

Some friends you better keep. Finally, my two
mentors and prayer warriors. Pastor Katisha
Spruill who encourages me all the way around,
as a sister, and friend that will call or text me
out of nowhere and check on me, advise,
support, prophecy a word, and will correct me
when I'm wrong in a heartbeat... I love her for
that and will say Iron sharpens Iron then say
love you talk soon! Bye! First Lady, Prophetess
Tina Bowden you have been a friend and a
sister and I thank God for you; you came in my
life toward the end and saw the hell I
encountered and endured in my life, a life of
the pain, hurt and embarrassment when I felt
like I was about to lose it...(emotionally and
spiritually) you and Pastor George. Thank you
for the endless and unselfish prayers, Thank
you for riding with me on road trips and
countless tears and laughter in the Lord as
well. May God continue to bless each one of
you in abundance In Jesus Name.

This book Is dedicated to those who had to deal or is dealing with any type of abuse. May God continue to give you peace, courage and strength in your journey path. Know that you have a voice and you are not alone; God is with you in every step that you take. (Hebrews 13:5 (KJV) says He will never leave you nor forsake you. You are to be loved and to be treated with dignity and respect. Continue to know your worth and know that you are special, you are (Psalms 139:14 KJV) fearfully and wonderfully made in God's image. Allow God to continue to lead and guide you step by step and If you haven't taken the first initial step to except Jesus into your heart as your personal Lord and Savior, I challenge you; today is the day to make that first step to a new journey. Don't put it off....(Rom; 10:9 KJV) confess with your mouth and believe in your heart that Jesus died on the cross for all of your sins, You don't have to wait to go to church, you can be at home, car, or even in a store. I personally know someone that did it at a beauty salon after work she asked me to drop her off, I waited with her for a while, God saw fit for me to wait; it was raining cats and dogs and afterwards her plan was to go to the club later that night and tell me about it .I use to talk to her about God all the time at work and she would listen and laugh, and then I would listen to her stories about her weekend

One thing with myself I will listen to you and give you respect because you want to be heard as well… see God has a way that's mighty sweet I remember staying the whole time with her and we was about to leave. I was on edge because I'm saying God you had me to stay the whole time and all she's talking about is the club and getting torn up…. Drinking! Well the beautician said something to her, then to myself and then I confirmed and said somethings and I remember hearing a loud and weeping sound and then hearing I need you Lord! I can't do this without you! I'm tired Lord! Help me God! See confessing is just talking to God no form or fashion, long or short asking God to forgive you for your wrongs your sins to make things right and to please him. talking to him like you talk to your friends or when you are on the phone about how much you love him and want a personal relationship with him, wanting him to save your soul. After surrendering your heart Instantly you are saved!! He doesn't renege on you or change his mind. That's how much he is in love with you. He excepts you for YOU! Now run and tell the good news that you are now saved (2 Cor 5:17) a new creature he will lead and guide you. The woman that I just spoke of is a close friend and now she and her husband are well known youth Pastors in Fayetteville, North Carolina.

Table of Contents

Step by Step Journey Writing Notes....

Step by Step Journey Notes............

Introduction

The Journey process for myself has never been easy since the day I came out of my mother's womb I struggled; I was told that when I was born, I had bronchitis, so it was hard for me to breathe.... (I am a June baby) and fighting in so many areas in my life of who I am, why I look the way I do, that sense of belonging, what people expect of me and what they think of me, and acceptance has been the most challenging. I thank God Almighty every day for his love and teaching me daily that he created me in his own image. it's a life process about myself and about others. In this journey some things I have learned and something I am taking the necessary steps of what I now call Embracing.... It's a journey step by step.

My mother was single raising us, and done the best that she could, I will never bash her to make her feel bad or even try to make her look bad, she is my mother at the end of the day. There are somethings that I will share because I have now learned to embrace truth and it's painful healing process, I've learned that my experiences are not just for myself and maybe to whomever may be reading this book that they too can relate and find or get the healing that they need, knowing that you are not alone.

I don't sing a song of woe it's me so I can get pity and all the stuff that goes with that. I'm me, learning continuously to grow; it doesn't matter how long or how slow the pace is as long I am taking steps to move forward step by step. My journey experiences have broken me and have brought me strength to be who I am today through all the things I did encounter as a child, teenager, and some things does explain a lot about myself as an adult today. My mom told me as a child that I would sit back and listen, and my eyes were big like quarters and I would just sit and look at people. I was always very quiet, and crowds have never been a big thing for me, isn't that something I'm a city girl but don't like crowds even today. There are times when I will shop for a bit but then I'm ready to go. Same as for church, and even social functions, I can be in a crowd, do what I need to do and will find a way of escape.

I don't always speak nor comment on everything, I love hard, but learned the hard way to let go of toxic people that are not beneficial for me or for my life. I can only help and do so much because God does the work and the saving, I'm just a willing vessel. There are a few people that I can truly call a friend and will stop doing what they are doing to pray and be there for me. I call them the few and faithful warriors! The rest I am beneficial only to them and that's being truthful. If I can help, be there, or go for them then everything is good. I stopped that and learned the hard way. I have always been very mindful about the things that I say because one thing I do know is pain, and hurtful words, we were taught at an early age that sticks and stones may break my bones, but words will never hurt me. That's a lie! The word of God says that there is life and death in the power of our tongue so the words that comes out of our mouths has power. (Proverbs 18:21 KJV) and the tongue is sharp it will cut you, Psalms 52:2 KJV) so when we speak out of our mouths its coming from the heart as well.

(Mathew 15:18 KJV) Words hurt and we carry those words with us like a purse and a wallet tucked away in our purses and back pockets. Think about those times when someone said you was not good enough or smart enough, that you will be like your mom or dad on drugs or in prison. I know what it felt like back then and what it feels like even today.

 Last year 2018 after going through some health issues is when God really showed me, I really began to examine people and even in my general surroundings. I had to have surgery, while in the hospital I had minor complications and a longer healing process; anyway. God had a selective few that when I say I needed help they were there, at the hospital and some at my house afterwards in and out and my small prayer circle afar that was long distance they would call, pray and intercede for and with me. I may have a small circle but mighty warriors in prayer!! I had two Aunties that got in the car and drove long distance and surprised me and made it their business because I was in so much pain and discomfort. I could hardly walk or eat. When you love you will go the distance no matter who or where you are. I didn't even look good. Many local friends would see a post here or there on social media and would say the right things like if you need anything let me know! I would tell them they would say I'm praying for you; I'm coming over and never showed up or would call and say I didn't forget about you and still never came over. I don't believe in tit for tat but when they needed me, I was there! I would just pray and cry; truthfully my feelings was so hurt because I know me, and I know my heart when it comes to people and how I treat people and I make myself available for everyone. I would go the distance if I had too but this time it was about me. I had to focus on me and getting well and see the bigger picture of what and who God was sending and then praying with no heart feelings towards anyone, pushing back darkness so God would get Glory. I can tell you this because of their hearts and obedience for helping me God blessed them and still opening doors for them and I thank God he sent me some faithful ones. (Angels) again I was in so much pain. I had stairs in my apartment, eighteen in counting and the kitchen was downstairs as well as the front door; some would call me an hour or two before coming so I could take my time to unlock the door. Many days I would be in tears trying to go down those stairs wishing I could stay downstairs, but I only had one bathroom and that was upstairs. I gave my kids grandmother a key because I knew if no one would ever come over it would be her. (smiling) again in so much pain, no work, on bed rest, limited to no driving because of the pain, I couldn't lay or sit too long but when I stood up with the staples in my stomach the tears would just fall out of my eyes. So, whenever I did get up to go to the rest room since I was already up, I would cry call on Jesus and slowly walk around my bedroom and pray. Normally when I would pray it would always be on my knees on the right side of my bed and in the dark, sometimes instrumental music and then I walked praying, declaring and decreeing or whatever he gave me to say or pray...

my favorite was in the shower, but I couldn't shower for about a week and two days (until follow up and removal) because the staples couldn't get wet. When I finally did shower the water would hit the wounded areas and I would be in tears... the healing process was a lot. I have a certain way at times at home with my Father but now it was a different way but the same Father.

 A month and a half passed with a little bit of relief but I still had another issue that needed attention and getting worse and my doctor was waiting for the healing process from surgery so I could be strong enough to really do for myself like drive, off meds and take care of this back issue I had. I had to get an MRI and had to start physical therapy. I had to go twice a week for almost 4 months, and did I mention twice a week also for allergy shots. Can I say limited activities and work so that meant a cut in hours at work and pay and I'm single and no extra income. When I tell you one thing after another! My kids' grandmother came by and took me too her house for about a week because she has a flat level house and easier for me to get around, I stayed and then went back to get staples removed.

One Friday night I got myself together and visited a friend church the man of God gave me a word and put the icing on the cake and confirmed things I had really been praying about for a while…. It was relieving and hurtful at the same time, but God is a God of love as well as for correction and wanted and allowed me to see their bad behaviors and correct myself. See if I could give my time, agreement, prayers, finances, events for church, and my Go…. We were all good, but the moment God began to sit me down and I really couldn't go, and my go now became NO! now there's a problem. Many even now think I am being funny or acting funny, I have lost people who I really thought that they genuinely loved me. It was manipulation and studying my character and what I could do for them and when people get familiar with you and think they really know you just get close and comfortable with some of your characteristics they feel like they can now mistreat you especially if you really don't say much like myself. I've learned that you are never too old to learn, we as parents also teach our children that if people are your friends, they will be there, and you won't have to question the friendship.

I now questioned even at this age about true friendship. It's sad but religious Christians can really manipulate people; they will turn it around and make it seem like it's now you. (you're the problem!) They would never allow someone else to mistreat them, but they will do it to you and don't see themselves as a manipulator why? because they are SAVED! I have encountered so many things and have learned that Christians won't admit or even say that they manipulate people.

There comes a time when we must take full responsibility of our actions. I often here the reasons why people don't want to go to church or don't want to be a Christian is because of how we interact and treat each other in the body of Christ. I will say this… you don't go to church for people, the purpose is to worship, reverence and have a personal relationship with God.

You may say well I can do it at home, true indeed and we thank God for having social medias and live stream has been a blessing when you are not able to go; the word says in Hebrews 10:25(JKV) Not forsaking the assembling of ourselves together, as the manner of some is; but exhorting one another; and so much the more, as ye see the day approaching. So, we are supposed to assemble ourselves ….

Therefore, we must go inside of the house of God to gain strength, fellowship and for us not to turn our backs on the church or the togetherness, to encourage one another and do good works.

I'm not against anyone nor am I here to bash people or Christians because I am a saved born again and a true believer of Jesus Christ. I must say as the body of Christ we need to do better and truly give and show Gods love not when we want too and when it is convenient for us. There are 2.18 billion beautiful Christians in this world that have the heart of Christ and I am one in a Billion.

Getting to know yourself..........

My Beginning

I remember at the age of 5 living on Vermont street in Brooklyn and riding a red tricycle, I don't know if it was mines or a friend on the block, my school was directly across the street from me P.S 182. I remember my first two teachers; their names were Ms. Lee and Ms. Perkins. I remember I got out of school @ 12 Noon and as soon as I got home I use to hear this theme music and then my mom talking back to the black and white T.V set with the two bunny ears sticking out talking about some man name Victor Newman, Nikki, and Mrs. Chancellor. Not realizing when I got older that was a soap opera called Young & The Restless. I started watching it when I was in high school (I loved Neal, Dru and Malcolm). We had our local corner store it was called Loco's my favorite thing in there was on this big high counter in a glass dish they were called Coconut Macron's I would always smile when I went in and Mr. Locko knew what I wanted, I would get it and close my eyes when I would take the first bite after eating it (smiling) Mr. Locko would laugh and say here's one more on me! Shh! Now get out of here waving his hand and laughing. There are some names on the block I do remember like Rodger, and a girl name Patty and vaguely something about a doll. We had some neighbors that spoke Spanish who played music with their window open all day long and they would be laughing on the stoop and dancing with drinks in their hands. They seemed to always be happy except one time there was a lot of yelling and arguing, they were speaking Spanish, shoving and raising their voices all of that took place while I was riding on my tricycle. I was going around and round and out of nowhere someone threw a glass bottle and a piece of it hit me and I got cut. I still have the scar on my right arm) My mom must have heard them yelling and came downstairs and grabbed me and took me inside to clean me up. My Uncle and his wife lived across the hall from us, they had a little brown puppy I use to try to touch her. I loved looking at animals but to touch them was a different story, but I would try. I just never been an animal person, my uncle would come across the hall and see us, later they would have a house party with my mom. As I am sitting back writing; so many childhood memories and flashbacks how times were safe and how times were very secretive, times have really changed for certain things. The phrase was said when I was growing up... Whatever happens in our house stay's in our house!! Things took place in people's houses you never knew what happened or things happened but were never talked about.

Private and Don't Tell

Not easy at the age of 6 we moved to Schenck Avenue that's still in Brooklyn. We lived in what they called a privately-owned building. We lived upstairs, and some neighbors lived downstairs it was an older lady Ms. P. and her grown daughter. My Big sister was in middle school, I was 6 and my younger sister was 4 years old. My mom and dad were together but things at an early age for us were very strange and dysfunctional like them arguing my mom did all the yelling, fussing, and cussing and I would always hear him say Rose go sit down and she would yell don't tell me to go sit down! Don't tell me what to do! we would be peeping through the door one time she grabbed his white T-shirt and torn it almost off of him and called the police, the police came and they went in our room and asked us if we was ok? then said he was going to check our closet. The police officer had a big black flashlight and a black stick, he looked in our closet and then said all clear then told us goodnight. We peeped and saw my dad was sitting in the chair and he explained what happened he was never high tempered nor a person to argue; he loved his chair with the pretty bow legs and thick plastic on it watching Karate flicks and Godzilla rocking back and forth drinking a beer but sitting for hours and trying to explain to us what he was watching. Again, both were drinking but he never put his hands on her but did tell the officer that he wanted to leave, and he left. About a week or so passed and he came back, and we thought that

everything was ok! remembering when he came back; she was at work and he was in the kitchen washing dishes, he's from Alabama and loved to cook he had cornbread in the oven. I came into the kitchen both my sisters were in the room but the bedroom door was right next to the kitchen and it was open and my mom came home spoke to him and she went to her room and came back in the kitchen and said that she needed to talk to him and he said ok! My mom tells him that she was leaving, and he says to go where? She said that she was going back to her home which is St. Thomas the Virgin Islands to marry my older sisters' father, he said ok! and continued washing the dishes and she packed and soon after left and married. When she got back, they talked as if everything was ok, but it wasn't, he stayed long enough to take care of us while she was gone, and he got his things and left. I was a child so not knowing why she did what she did it was told in our adult lives that she still was in love with my eldest sisters father and the heart wouldn't let go of him but in all of that he promised her to come back to the states but he never did. So, she lost on both ends. Again, we were all young, but we remembered what happened just didn't know why and what effects it had on us and even later in life.

My sister and I would go outside all the time. One time my younger sister and I went outside to play, and we got a pot of water and threw it in the air to get wet and it literally started raining; we just knew we made it rain. (laughing) Running inside saying we made it rain! We made it rain!

We met a nice older couple that lived next door to us Mr. & Mrs. Gray they probably were in their late 50's they invited us over and had beautiful black and white pictures when they were younger and of Mr. Gray when he was in the Army. They lived downstairs and her daughter, son in-law and grandkids lived upstairs. They had owned the house; that was the first time I had ever known for someone black to own a house. I was only 6 but we always lived in an apartment. They would invite us over to their back yard because they had a grape vine with the biggest grapes I ever saw, they would tell us to take as much as we wanted and some days Mrs. Gray would wait for us to come outside and play and she would have some grapes in a bowl wrapped up for us to eat for later.

My older sister she was gone a lot for school stuff and going to her grandmother's in the Bronx. Remembering times when my mom would be friendly and go down stairs and she would speak to the neighbors, the landlord was an older woman and by momma working with elderly people she took on to her, back then momma was a certified home attendant, now they call them CNA's. While momma took on to helping Ms. P her daughter took on to me... I guess since I was always quiet, I didn't talk a lot. I never did anything extra for either of them. There were times she would call me downstairs to help her and her mom get or do things in their apartment. My mom would tell me to go and help they are nice people. It's ok! you can go!

 I never thought differently until she had me to do inappropriate things and then say.... don't tell then it was .... you better not tell and threatening me!

 I Just tried to forget about it; and pretend it never happened, my mother never told us about people touching you and your private areas are never to be touched by anyone male or female. She only said don't talk to strangers and never go with a stranger anywhere! Run and Scream! I guess that was supposed to be taught later. The older I got of course with full understanding about right and wrong, sexuality, your body and violating someone and morality; the embarrassment of being violated by a woman and shame started to set in, the sad thing is that you never forget only God helps with the internal scars, hurt, and embarrassment and it is a healing process. When you are young like that you don't know any better and it's not your fault....

I carried so much for years, but they are the ones with a serious problem that's rooted in them and they truly need God and professional help.

We visited New York years later I was grown, and my mother wanted to visit all the old neighborhoods. Many of them she kept in contact with over the years, so my mother and I went to see Mrs. Gray she was now in her late 70's and Mr. Gray went on home to be with the Lord. She had the same pictures in the same spot just like when I was 6... She said that her daughter and kids had moved to the south, I believe it was Georgia. Ms. P had died also but her daughter still lived their... Mrs. Gray showed me outside where the grapes use to be, she said she couldn't maintain them like she use too and especially after Mr. Gray passed, she said it was like the grapes had passed too. She talked about how much they loved one another, and they had married at seventeen. Then she asked about my younger sister (my sister had a way with words!) and shook her head and just laughed! We all laughed! I told her she was doing very well. We told her how great it was to see her and gave our hugs then Mrs. Gray held my hands looking at me and was just smiling and I gave her another hug and we left; as my mother and I was talking about how great Mrs. Gray looked, we was walking down the street headed to another one of our old neighborhoods (Miller Avenue.) and my mother says the person's name Oh my goodness!!!!! Glenda you know who this is? We approached her, Ms. P daughter my mom said I'm sorry to hear Mrs. Gray just told me that your mom passed away! Yes Ms. Rose! Then she said hi Glenda… and put her head down then holding this little boy's hand and said this is my son. I was abrupt and said momma let's GO! I began to feel like a child for a moment but scared, then anger and now my heart thumping and I want to cry and fight…That feeling of rage that is unfamiliar but felt like I had every reason to feel this way, I said yelling at my mom for the first time ever in my life YOU TALK! I CAN'T!!!, YOU STAND HERE AND TALK TO HER! I

DON'T EVER WANT TO SEE NOR TALK TO HER.... NEVERTHELESS, SAY HI. I was saying this as I'm walking off.... momma, she knows what she did to me she knows what she use to do to me.... My mom saying Glenda! what?? She left her standing their.... I waited on the end of the corner for my mom. What happened? What's going on? What in the world is going on? so, I told her what she done to me. I told her Everything!!!!!!! She wanted to go back.... NO! for what! She knew when she saw me momma, she just thought that she would never see me again! God allowed that! That's why she couldn't look me in my face... Saying to my mom that's her guilt she's walking around with, her problem and filth, she's the one who must answer to God... I was six years old momma! Six... first grade. It was so painful and emotional for me to see her but hurtful for my mom because she never knew and didn't know what was going on. I carried that with me for years of why she chose and did those things to me and now she has a child, a son and truth be told boys are not exempt from being molested. I would never want a child to ever have to experience that ever. I pray that she; along with many other molesters preying on innocent children that they seek professional help.

19

A Taste of Church

Let's Rewind back for a moment to allow you to know that I wasn't always in the church nor saved, Most children have had a parent or parents in the church and you had to go with them, or they sent you and they never went with you. When I was a little girl, I remember going a couple of times with my neighbors in the building where we lived in Brooklyn now living on Wynona Street. I am now 8 years old. I also remember going to church with my big sister to B.T.B Church in the Bronx on the weekends when she would visit her grandmother, One time I had to memorize a part for an Easter play they were having; my sister signed me up and I was terrified, I already spoke soft and didn't talk a lot, very shy and I hated getting up in front of people even today… That's something how the very thing you don't like, and you may even hate ends up being the very thing God may have you to do... Again, I did not want to do this at all and on top of that my sister never even asked me if I wanted to do this. I believe they gave me like three weeks to learn the part. One thing about church as I remembered;

there were a lot of old people a lot of them was nice, and many were very mean and had lots of rules. Like no eating candy! But the adults ate peppermint. I'm thinking that was candy!! NO mistreating others that was a sin! but you would see the old people pulling kids by their ears or pinching them! Some things as a child didn't make sense to me. But if you asked me to go to church, I would go. So, I went to the Easter play my sister had to guide me, she took me by my hand and walked me to the front of the pulpit and said you can do it. I was so scared… They gave me a microphone, I was so terrified that I would forget my lines, I opened my mouth, and nothing came out at first and then finally I said my part.

"Jesus loves the little children in that land so far away and I'm so very glad he loves us on this Happy Easter Day!"

Yes, I did it! They all applauded, and grandma Reid and my sister were so proud yelling yeah!!! I told you that you could do it!

We Never Knew

One time my younger sister and I went to
church with our mother, she had choir
rehearsal, prior to going; we never even knew
that she even went to church to even be in any
one's choir….anyway we went in the church
and she sat us down to get us settled. I was
about eight years old and my younger sister
was now six. My mom was going to what I now
know is called a balcony! On the balcony there
was a lot of men and women in these bulky
long big robes and this short man up in the
front of all the people waving his arms and all
the people following his directions and
instructions while singing…..(Choir director)
they called him Mr. Bay. She put on her robe
and as soon as they started to sing my sister
yells out MA……. I GOTTA PEE!!!

My mom came down from the choir stand, she
was so mad, she came down and took my
sister to the bathroom, then took off her robe,
told me to come on; she threw her robe across
her arm, we all left the church and never
returned.

As I stated in the beginning not easy…Like
many others we all have a story; we all have
gone through something. There are going to be
times we may or may-not be able to discuss or

share with others, I've learned that the things I have encountered is not just for me but for others as well. I'm not going to say that it was easy but never be ashamed of what you have gone through. There will come a time in your life that you will learn to embrace and cast your cares upon the Lord because he truly cares for you. 1 Peter 5:7 KJV) Never stop treating people right because they treated or did you wrong. Continue to show Godly love and allow his light to shine through you.

I've learned now that I am saved through the blood of Jesus Christ, I have accepted him as my personal Savior; I see things in a totally different perspective, and I thank God for new. (2 Cor 5:17) (JKV).

A City Girl

As a Brooklyn city girl, you learn many things, and quick! In my time you went outside and played with your friends for hours at a time. There was never the statement I'm bored, or I don't want to go outside. There was so much to do for example, we played Double Dutch, Freeze Tag, Hopscotch, Handball on the corner where the cleaners were, Jacks on the stoop, Kick the Can, Skelly and the boys sometimes tossing a Football in the middle of the street. One summer I will never forget two of the boys on my block was tossing the ball and I said I want to play; "I want to catch the ball" Go play some Double Dutch or something! Please I want to catch the ball and I won't ask again, Poppy said okay! (I really liked Poppy) but Evo was the one who threw the ball. He told me to go long waving his hand for me to go further away from him; then told me stop and then he threw the ball and it was a long throw.... I don't think he purposely meant to throw it that far, hard or fast. I guess boys really don't know their own strength because he did! and long behold; I caught it .... right in the middle of my stomach and it knocked the wind right out of me. (laughing now sipping on my lemon green tea) they came flying down the street and I'm on the ground with a football. They asked me if I was-okay? again, are you alright? Explaining they didn't mean to throw it that hard and they didn't really think I was going to catch it…. yea I'm okay! Holding my stomach looking at poppy with a half-smile, half pain looks on my face. They helped me up and told me to go back down the block before Ms. Rose kills us!

On our block everyone knew each other, and neighbors was constantly on the lookout! You can say they were nosey and knew if you belonged on the block or not and if you were doing something you had no business let's just say you got a double portion. Yes, a village and a community. (Laughing) All the kids loved summer break when we got to play in the water and the adults would open the fire hydrant for all the kids. Oh! how we loved that!! We called the fire hydrant The Johnny Pump! The cops would come on our block; well… anyone's block and turn the water off, they didn't want it on they would say that we had a water shortage and turn the water off with a wrench and just as soon as they left one of the adults would turn it right back on and say ….now you kids play and have fun!!! then someone would get a can so we could make a waterfall the can had to be open on both ends to make a waterfall. Back then we were very creative and used our imagination and creativity not like children today stuck in the house barely going outside to play, they rather play on I pads and video games for hours never stimulating their minds for the outside world and life.

We had video games like Centipede, Millipeede, Space Invaders, MS. Pac Man, Popeye, and Mario Brothers but; we had to go to the corner store or the game room, and if you did; that was a treat! Because times and money were hard for us, but we played outside all day long and everyone wanted to go outside and play no matter what time of day or year it was. We were not allowed to go in and out all-day! especially days when we did get wet, you were not going to wet up momma's wooden Parcay floors. She didn't play that! Now that I am thinking about it none of the parents played that either you stayed in or you stayed out. By evening time, the parents would come out and sit on the stoop and talk and some of the girls would get their hair braided and listen to music. Back then kids never sat around grown folks and was never in grown folk conversations unless we were asked, if company came over, we had to go to our room. It was called respect as well as stay in a child's place. We had a neighbor on our block we would have so much fun there was a man on our block name Mr. Stacy; everyone knew him, he lived on the second floor he lived right next door to us, his window was facing towards the front right next to the building where we lived and he would throw all sorts of change out of his window for all the kids on our block, I guess as a treat and he would see some kids with and some without snacks; so he would stick his head out the window when he got off work and before you knew it; change would be all over the ground and all the kids picking it up and flying down the street to get to the corner store. Some would get the long icy some Italian icy in the cup. Many times, we would get penny candy and I would save mines till later or whenever I decided to eat it, I loved Shoestrings, Swedish Fish, Mary Jane, Boston Baked Beans and Now & Later. When I finally would open and start to eat my candy and my sister would ask for some because hers was gone... I would get a beating for not sharing even though we all had equal amounts and she had her own just like I did. I would get so upset and cry because it was not fair and If I did that to her my mom would say; you had your own!! Glenda NO!! My siblings and I didn't have an easy life even though there may have been favoritism against one another all of us suffered in ways that was very painful and still to this day as adults resides within us.

I am the middle girl that was hard for me, my older sister was gone a lot and I was responsible for my younger sister because my mom did have to work. We were latch key kids and had chores like many but if my sister didn't do her chores I would get a beating, remembering I was told to get my hair braided and when I went to get my hair braided and the girl Theresa took too long I got a beating. Growing up I was called stupid and told that I sound stupid with my black self and told by my mom that she wished that I was never born. I always felt so different and treated differently.... But why? There were times I was treated differently because I was quiet(was stupid) and my skin color was different from my siblings...Before my grandfather (mothers father) passed away I remember him always playing the harmonica he had very fair skin like my mom could almost pass for Caucasian and his hair... he would put grease and water and it would curl up instantly. He would say either your light or your white. I was young but I remembered. Thinking now how she was raised is how she raised us and because I was the dark one I seriously payed for it.....beatings for no reason, abusive words, because of her pain and anger for whatever she dealt with, so it was easier for her to see me as the target.

Between the siblings there's an age difference no more than 9years from the oldest to the youngest, they all saw or knew how my mother showed a difference and how she handled me even today as a grown woman.

There were times when some of my friends would notice; for instance, one girl on our block she stayed across the street from us. Leslie, we called her Sheree she was always in all my classes with me every year when we went to P.S 13 she asked me why my younger sister would get new clothes? and I didn't? Why does your mom yell at you all the time? I would make up things and excuses like she had a bad day at work but, on the inside, I asked the same thing. I would cry at night with my head under the covers and say why is she so mean to me? and don't like me? why she pays more or gives more attention to my sisters? There is nothing worse than feeling like your mother doesn't love you!

Write down some things that you love about yourself.......

WHY?

During summer vacation I asked my mother why my sister always got new clothes? and got to go to Alabama? I would ask why can't I go? I Never got full answers and there was always an excuse of there was no room in the car for me. So, I always stayed behind in tears and told... Glenda go back outside and play. When she would come back her suitcase would be filled with new clothes, socks, underwear and dresses all for the upcoming year for school. For me was nothing!! I would get my older sister's hand me downs or the neighbor's old stuff they would give to me because sometimes I would babysit for them for about an hour or two. I had never received new; I made the best out of a bad situation. I always wanted my sister to be with me we practically did everything together, often we use to sneak in our older sisters' room on the weekends and play detective and use her dresser drawers. We would pretend that they were file cabinets, trying to find clues. Two of the drawers had a bunch of her old school papers, many of the papers had old grades on them. The grades that were circled were clues! Many Times, when we use to pretend to play grown up and say we was going to marry, and our husbands last names was going to be Davenport... because it sounds rich! We used to see a huge white 18-wheeler truck drive down our street with blue letters Davenport. Then we would sneak and put on momma's high heels and get my mom's wine glasses and put water in it or whenever we had Kool-Aid (laughing that was white and red wine) and toast and say cheers! like we were grown but having so much fun. I hated so many things and had questions to why my mom treated me so much differently from my siblings and there were times they knew this what could they do, My older sister would come get me for the weekends and take me to the Bronx with her just so I wouldn't get in trouble or a beating but the older I got the worse she became… I never stopped loving her. I was always longing for my mother's love again; not easy when you want to be loved and excepted; but treated like an outcast. So, I always had questions in my mind as a child and to God when I got older…. of Why?

Rough

My mom worked but it was hard and had very little of anything many times we were without lights, or food, I remember saving food from the summer free lunch program so my sister and I would eat later when we got home, summer time we had free lunch so I would eat some and save some and take it home for later to share with my sister.. Sometimes free lunch closed at a certain time and they made a certain amount of bag lunches so the number of children would vary, so sometimes they would make too many or some kids may not come that day so I would stick around till the end and sometimes they would give me extra bag lunches so they wouldn't have to throw it in the trash, you talk about happy... especially when they would do that and it was a Friday we would have more for the weekend. During the holidays especially Christmas time I remember us always having a live tree smelling like fresh pine, momma would get it on credit from Locko's store but when it came to having presents under the tree that was a different story; so my younger sister and I would swop old things out with one another like if my teacher gave me a book and I knew she would like it I would wrap it with newspaper from the funny papers, back then we use to get Archie, and Charlie Brown along with other characters that escapes my mind at this moment, and she knew I loved socks So I would get socks, we helped and looked after one another. One year our Eldest sister brought us a pair of ice skates we were so excited I had one blade and my sister had two blades. I guess my sister thought that was a good present at the time because it was different, but we never used them…. We couldn't afford to go to Rockefeller Center that was in Midtown Manhattan, we lived in Brooklyn that was train fare that momma did not have and the least of her worries she had to work, and weekends was her time and made that very clear.(Eventually we outgrew them) There were many times on weekends when my mom had the house parties, music, drinking with her loud friends and neighbors, My mom knew I love to sing and dance I wake up I would sing I would even make up songs by myself and I always loved older music…. There were so many times being told to shut up! But then there were times she would call me out the room and I would sing a song or two I sang Let Me Be Your Rocking' Chair and I'll Take You There! And my most favorite song of all, I

Wanna Rock with You, by Michael Jackson
then go back to the room with my sister
watching TV. My younger sister's father whose
now my dad use to watch us perform and sing
Love Will Keep Us Together,

and We Are Family he would sit there and
listen to us from arranging songs to
choreography, I always wanted to be in the
front and sing We are Family like Kathy in the
sister group. It was always something about
her and she seem so happy and pretty to me.
That's the only time I ever wanted to ever be in
front of anyone for anything but, my Eldest
sister was "Diana Ross" telling us what to do!
Being in the middle to me was again very
difficult but seems as if I was on the end, I
really began to feel I had no place. I never
hated my siblings despite how I was treated. I
just always had that sense of why am I here? I
didn't ask to be born, I didn't ask to be
mistreated (tears) why am I being punished
because I am dark skin, tall, crooked teeth and
skinny?, all my siblings are lighter than me
and short like everyone on her side of the
family in St Thomas, why am I told to shut up
all the time when I hardly talk? and being
called black?. The older I got the less I talked
and the more I became very withdrawn I've
always felt out of place Why? because If she
as a mother felt this way about me her own

child and told me in my face surely others felt that way about me too. I was never enough in her eyes; I was never good enough and a mistake and I carried this with me even in my adulthood.

A Summer Invite

My mother had a God son back from her home St. Thomas, VI we knew nothing about him, His mother had contacted momma and told her that he was having problems in school skipping and smoking ganja (weed) So his mother sent him and he came to live with us until he graduated high school that upcoming year... I was about 10 or 11years old. My oldest sister is now about to graduate high school, she now permanently lived with her grandmother in the Bronx and was going off to college, her room was now promised to me the room where we use to play detective in, oh boy!! I had never had my own room before. Now told my room becomes his, instead of bunking me and my sister together my mom gives this perfect stranger the room and we are now Michael and JJ on the couch. I was so crushed, my mom told us to be nice to him and make him feel at home, show him around, that he's family and far from home. Well after months passing by, he got settled with school which was Thomas Jefferson High school and routine with household chores and how we did things, he would show me how the boys would play marbles in St. Thomas. I would laugh he would start to tickle me and from tickling he began to fondle me, and I told him I was going to tell my mother, he would say that it was an accident he didn't mean it and it became more frequent then touching me at night and putting his hand over my mouth many times he would jack me on the wall and say he was going to beat me up and put his fist in my face....I would be so scared! Every time I was going to tell he would put his finger on his lips (Shh!) with his fist balled up getting ready to punch me in my face. I remember we moved to Miller Avenue. My mom always made us wash out our panties at night while we would take a shower so we could keep clean under clothes. One night he was in the room I had just got in the bed to watch tv before curfew was up and he came across in the room stuck his hands under the covers and was fondling me. I made a noise and hit the wall my mom got up but never came in she stood at her doorway and said what yawl doing in there? He put his hand over my mouth holding me down because she never came in and he said quickly Nothing God mother Rose!!! I thought I heard something, Glenda... Turn that tv off!! And told him goodnight! She was walking back to her room, he said OK! he put both his hands around my neck and said IF YOU EVER TELL!

He got up and went to the living room that's where he slept but the Tv was in my room my sister and I shared the room but most times she slept in the room with my mom and summers she was in Alabama. I was so terrified…. He would walk around the house and talk to my mom as if nothing ever happened and smile at me. He finally graduated high school and his mother sent for him to go back. I never told or said anything until I was grown and of course everything was denied as if nothing never happened, my mom spoke to his mother and she said it never happened, but my mom never spoke to him to see what happened. My mother did ask me why I never said anything, and I told her about the threats and abuse and I said to her whenever I try to talk to you; you would always tell me that I sound stupid and to shut my black mouth! She said nothing it was total silence and that was the end of that for her; but pain for me I was that at 6-year-old terrified threatened and molested again and now this time this person is supposed to be family…. my Godbrother.

Addition to The Family with No Explanations!

I met my Oldest brother for the first time at the age of 12, my first birthday celebration ever. It was me, both my sisters my mom and my dad. I got a finger paint set from my oldest sister. We all went outside on the stoop and I asked who is that boy? he doesn't live on this block or in our building? and my mom said smiling.... that's your brother!!! he spoke to our oldest sister first and gave her a hug and said hello to us and then we all went upstairs. He lived in St. Thomas the Virgin Islands. Meanwhile we were all born in New York City, for my birthday he took me on the Staten Island ferry for the first time, I got sick from the motion of the boat. He asked me what I wanted for my birthday and I told him. He was taking me to buy my first pair of roller skates I wanted a pair like Tootie on the facts of life. When we got their because it was a military base I could not go inside because I didn't have I.D (disappointed) so he brought me back home and apologized and asked me what else I wanted for my birthday name it! and I told him a box of

Frosted Flakes cereal not Corn Flakes even
though I use to love getting the Jackson 5
stickers out of the regular box. I guess he went
to the corner store and came back and gave
me a big box of Frosted Flakes, and money
$10.00 to buy whatever I wanted. He nor
momma never explained to us where he been
until really …. when we all were grown piecing
things and stories together, He was raised by
his grandparents in St. Thomas VI.

My First True Friendship

My first best friend was James {Jimmy} we met at about age 10 he was 11 we were like two peas and a pod.

Our parents are good friends even today, my mom at the time was dating his mom's cousin Al. Back then the parents would get together and have house parties the adults played records, played cards, drank, talk and the kids played in the room. On Easter weekend Jimmy's parents would always have an Easter egg hunt inside their apartment, it was so much fun and there were times he would find the eggs with the candy and give it to me; I didn't like the real eggs. The parents really enjoyed watching us laughing and hunting even though it was in the apartment it seemed like we were outside. When we were finished, he would give me all his candy Now & Later were my favorite. Then we would talk for hours while the adults did there thing and then he would rap. He loved music like Doug E Fresh, Boogie Down productions, Eric B and Rakim and many others. Then I learned some rap music. One summer I will never forget my sister and I went to our local park called Gershwin Park and WBLS came and Doug E. Fresh was there, I guess it was for promotion and he was rapping, and I got to dance with Doug E. Fresh for a few minutes what a memorable moment.

My sister and I talk about that from time to time when we reminisce. It's kind of reminds me like the movie Brown Sugar before it was even a movie. (smiling) During the summer our parents would go to Central Park and Prospect Park and have cookouts... We would laugh and talk then Jimmy showed me how to skip rocks on the water... I guess that's what boys do showing off. (laughing) I remember our first kiss and gave me a ring out of the cracker jacks box saying I was his girl and I was going to marry him. (laughing) I was his girl, but we never married I moved to NC. We kept in contact. I did not return home until after I graduated high school... That's when I got my first job working for American Express that summer we hooked up and it was like I never left New York City and reminiscing and spending time like when we were younger. He would ride the train from Brooklyn to come see me because I was staying in Harlem with my auntie just like old times, when he would walk all the way from my house to his, or walk me home and then walk all the way back to his. Now young adults riding trains for transportation. I returned to North Carolina because my mom had surgery and she had a heart attack during the procedure. Jimmy and I remain best friends even today, He has a beautiful wife and children.

Times Are Truly Changing

The summer of 1985 My oldest sister was now married and, in the USMC, and had her first child Christopher Jr. My first Nephew…. She wanted me to come for the summer and watch him because she did not want him in daycare as a first-time mom, so I came July 15,1985 that was the first time I ever got on a plane and left Brooklyn, New York. Little did I know a summer vacation would turn into a permanent move. I left my best friend Jimmy and other friends with no goodbyes or anything! That fall was my first year of High School it was very awkward for me, when the average is out dating boys, doing social stuff I was in doing what I loved best playing with my nephew, watching TV like Sanford and Son, Cosby show, Different World, and singing, Whitney Houston, and listening and dancing to Michael and Janet Jackson, New Edition, later on was Salt N Peppa, Kid N Play and Boyz to Men. I began to get some friends, but I was never a social butterfly I left that to my younger sister, we are sisters and totally different, to me she was a little bolder and social. she fit in more with people than me, I was very quiet, reserved and still today. New York City and North Carolina was totally a different world…. No more sitting on the stoop it's now called a porch, they have these bugs that rub their legs together and makes a noise that is called a cricket, that you hear all night long and disrupts your sleep you may be saying she's from New York City the city that never sleeps and noise all the time. Trust me it's different and I didn't like it at all. NO double Dutch, handball, hop-scotch or skelly in the middle of the street, What?! No block parties!!... music is a noise ordinance if it's too loud! I stated I am a quiet person but this... was TOO MUCH! This may sound weird, but I liked going to school but I felt like school didn't like me…. I was tall and very skinny, crooked teeth…I didn't have what a lot of the other girls had but mind you I wasn't doing what many of the girls were doing to get it either. Guys wanted a certain look some of the guys I was taller than, most wanted the challenge of a tall girl only to get what they wanted and report back to others, and some I thought that I liked was taken and or I'm good enough only to be their homie to hook them up with what friends I did have. I knew a lot of guys that would speak and most only by name of what we called high school popularity.

I had two guys that I had a crush on for years one was two years ahead of me, and the other the same year as me, when I finally would go out with some of my friends to a local teens club called Jams or go to the mall, (hang out spot) I would see him, and my heart would be in my throat! he would be surrounded around all his football buddies and the popular ones. So, NO CHANCE! I would speak, most times I said nothing…. Finally, one night I was at the local teens club Jam's on the floor dancing with the girls and we all came together, we could do that back in the day without someone thinking differently! We would dance with someone and turn around and switch and anyone could be dancing in front of you, Well I turned around and there he was… Feet don't fail me now. I Never forgot that day! We became good friends throughout the year's truth is we had a little history years down the road, we remain to be friends even today and reminisce every now and them, but ladies never be with someone that you must hide and can't and won't be seen with in public. No, he never married, but a jewel or diamond wants to be showed off from time to time: if not then you will feel like you are placed in a position as if you're not good enough.

He introduced me to football every now and then we corresponded from time to time and discuss our favorite football team; there was a time he was there for me through some rough patches in my life that happened to me later down the years, but sometimes close friends are not always meant to be in a relationship. As far as the other crush we are also good friends. I never mentioned to him that was years ago and he is happily married and has children.

The transition between New York City and North Carolina was never easy for my sister or me, our adaptability from the city to the south was one thing but our living environment was something totally different, we went from bad to worse. When it was initially supposed to be a move for the better. Behind closed door we lacked in many areas and suffered in so many ways, in the beginning was ok because we had a support system and that was our older sister who now had her own family but was there for us. She would buy us school clothes and school supplies, she worked in supply in the USMC she would ask permission first before she brought stuff home. Then she would come home and walk over to our apartment and gave us everything we needed. One time I remember my younger sister and our friend came over to our apartment she stayed across the street from us her mom and our mom became very good friends; anyway my mother was at work since they were like family now it was ok for her to come over even if momma was at work. Anyway, this day her and my sister decides to bring extra friends at the house... boys for that matter! Remember I told you my sister was more outgoing than me, I'm very quiet and laid back and don't like trouble. I was scared to death and to bring me into this; they went and got a neighborhood boy who liked me but I had no interest in at all, so I send him back home and they get another boy for me who wore braces name Jay and let the boys in… Again, scared to death and I want them out!! My older sister happens to come over to check on us to see if we needed anything of all days! remember momma was at work and she knocks on the door it's me open the door!

I'm about to cry my eyes already big now looking like silver dollars and scared. These two laughing and shoving boys in closets and went and sat down like it was nothing! Telling me to shut up and open the door! I opened the door and my sister says what took so long? It's three of yawl in here! I guess the Holy Ghost, discerning spirit done told because out of nowhere my sister gets up and says what's going on and whose here?! She goes straight to the closet in the living room and the bedroom closet! GET OUT! GET OUT NOW!!! Even she left! (Laughing) Boy you talk about big time trouble. I got on punishment for 2 weeks and extra chores and my sister had 1 week because I was supposed to set the example even though they brought the boys to the house, not sure if our friend got in trouble or not by bringing them to our apartment but they stayed doing and getting into something. As time progressed, I made another friend she was very popular in school but not the popularity I wanted and the kind that whispered in school. We hung out and she stayed over once or twice, she was the kind of friend she was so funny, knew a lot of boys but too fast for me; but cool as a person. She would introduce me to boys, but I had no problem of saying No! or I'm not ready for all of that! One time she spent the night and called some boys over late at night they tapped on my bedroom window and she began to talk to them, brought one over for me had a jerry curl. I had remembered that incident with my sister and made them leave ASAP. Meanwhile my sister met a boy from another Highschool that had his own car an orange Pinto and sometimes would let us drive his car around only in the neighborhood, so he could spend time with my sister and she's was sneaking him in the house or she would go to his house all the way in Richlands a 30 minute drive and nothing ever said. Then I'm asked where is your sister? I don't know but saying to myself you're the mom and you don't know where your child is?! And I would get in trouble and put on punishment! When she would come back it was never a big thing. My older sister I won't forget her saying to our mother don't you need to ask her where she's been? and our mother's response was mind your business!!! she's not doing anything! he's a nice boy I like him. There's no harm!

My sister was mad and said this is crazy one gets in trouble all the time for nothing and the other one running loose, and nothing is said! I'm minding my business and I'm going back to

my apartment! then momma said good!! Few
weeks passed my older sister still never came
back over and my younger sister got her first
period and no clue of what to do crying, scared
she just said she wanted it to stop; I explained
to her what was going on and then went to my
sister's house to get some sanitary napkins
because we ran out. My sister was so hurt she
only wanted the best for us. Shortly after my
sister left and got orders to Quantico VA things
really changed for us and began to spiral and
go downhill. I remember when I began to start
making friends at school and a friend of mines
had a class with me and we had a test coming
up and she suggested that we study together
over the weekend my mom said ok so her
mom dropped her off and she got there and we
stayed outside for a while and then we walked
to the seven-eleven walking and talking and
showed her the neighborhood pool and came
back and my mom told me in private that the
lights got turned off so we played it off and I
told her that my mom got called in for the
weekend and there would be no supervision so
her mom needed to come pick her up and she
said how about I stay over her house?. Her
mom came and then asked my mom was it
alright while I stayed the weekend if I could go
to the mall with them and ride the bus for
Monday at their house with my friend to school
and ride my bus for the afternoon as a way to
come back home since she had to work on
Sunday and couldn't bring me back. . My mom

said that was fine. I really had fun studying that was my first time studying with a friend and learned a lot and enjoyed my friend company and her family we both had totally different back grounds but that never mattered I just liked having a new friend and not so wild. The lights were off for about a week, again people never know behind closed doors what other people go through. We began to get more friends We moved to another area and a lot more people that I would see from school lived in that neighborhood. There were so many times we didn't even have lights or food. Many of the friends never knew. As time progressed things really got bad for us. My sister got pregnant with my nephew. I was in the room when she took the test and now had to tell her that she was pregnant. I remember the family meeting and the conversation and words, with both being young, Time progressed and then my mom said she was leaving to go back to New York to work and make money because they didn't pay enough money in North Carolina so the plan was to get caught up on bills and come back. My mother left us the whole summer by ourselves, no phone, no money, the little food we did have ran out, then the electricity got turned off and a pregnant sister who was now 7 to 8 months. I tried the best I could, we both were in high school honestly; I knew nothing about going out to get a job that was never even taught to me. I was about to be a junior in high school.

That whole summer I was trying to fend for me and my sister to get us food to eat through my friends, Finally my sisters baby fathers, mother found out and took my sister to go stay with them until my mom got back, for us we had no idea of when she was coming back. So, I was left in an apartment to myself and no supervision nor provision. I Then started to learn how to hang out with my friends so I could eat and wouldn't have to be by myself alone and in the dark. I went to a party and met a boy name Mike he was quiet, tall, and fine. We hit it off he was from NJ. He told me that he was watching me all night and had to find out who I was and where I was from. We hit it off great, He would come by and spend time with me eventually I told him what was going on and he would sneak food from his mom's house and bring it to me. I met his mom and siblings they were all cool, sometimes she would ask me to stay for dinner and of course I didn't refuse. Mike never told her what was going on. Mike had a driver's license so sometimes he would borrow his mom's car and we would go to the park and spend time together and sometimes his mom would drop him off for a while. We really hit it off.

A note to yourself:

The Father created you; therefore, you are good enough. There are going to be times in your life when you have wondered what and how did some things happen. Most things we put on ourselves and some is just God… but remember that the Devil is out to kill, steal, and destroy John 10:10 (KJV) he also thinks that he has his own plan as well, but he is a liar and we are more than a conqueror through him that loved us.

Romans 8:37(KJV). It's just a reminder in and for your life. Despite the many things that I have encountered, or you may encounter, I still trust and thank God for everything because it is for my making. (Jeremiah 29:11 NIV) For I known I have plans for you Declares the Lord plans to prosper you not to harm you, plans to give you hope and a future. He gets Glory for everything! It may be hard but embrace the plans and the process. I fought for so many years and somethings are still a learning and healing process, the process to except what is …. Is and what's not…NOT. Of course, if I could have changed a lot of things I would have, and somethings were nowhere in my control and it began to manifest in my life, to the point that even late in my age I had to embrace this to become and be who I am today. Right now, in your life it may seem hard but know that Jesus loves you and has not forgotten about you. It's part of the journey process (Deuteronomy 31:8 NIV) says The Lord himself goes before you and will never leave you nor forsake you, do not be afraid; do not be discouraged. So continue to hold on to him and thank him for the process, Yes you will cry and hurt, and I'm not going to paint you this picture that life is easy and once you give your life to Christ that all your troubles will magically disappear and you will never have problems ever again, I can tell you that God is with you and the pain and troubles doesn't last always. (Psalms 30:5) Weeping may endure for a night but joy cometh in the morning .You may feel like you can't do it… Truth is you can, continue to press and try him, give him a chance open up your heart and receive him, Things will begin to unfold, your life does matter and will change but for the better. He has a plan for each one of us. (1Peter 5:10) But the God of all grace who hath called us unto his eternal glory by Christ Jesus, after that ye have suffered a while, make you perfect, stablish, strengthen, settle you.

Hold on and continue to keep the faith knowing that God is just who he says that he is, and he is a man that shall not lie, He is faithful and has greatness for your life.

Inspiration

A <u>Dream</u> that is written down with a date on it becomes a <u>Goal.</u>

A <u>Goal</u> that is broken down into steps becomes a <u>Plan.</u>

A <u>Plan</u> that is backed by action becomes a <u>Reality.</u>

Write down some of your own personal goals.

Special Notes to Yourself...................

Love And in love

We know that there is a difference between loving someone and being in love with someone. I met the perfect man beautiful person, eyes like marbles, caring, picky eater, loving, respectful, protector and loved me for me, and made me laugh all the time, never scared to show his emotions. We laugh and cried on the phone as well as in one another's arms.

He was in the USMC Camp Geiger where I lived, I met him through a mutual former classmate, she use to drive taxi cabs and drive all the Marines (Boots) straight out of boot camp with no cars around and said they all had friends they wanted to meet since they all were new to the area and now stationed here....
She passed the word to us so later we all met and introduced ourselves, hung out and it went from there. Honestly, I really didn't party or got out much I guess that's why she told me. We hit it off spending time together every time and every chance he got he was right at my front door.

We were still kind of young, carefree... going out to the park, partying a little at a friend house getting to know and teaching one another. On weekends he would get liberty passes and come off post to come be with me and when he would take leave he would go to his home town and then come back home to Jacksonville to be with me for a couple of days before he would have to report back to base. Time progressed and we established a beautiful relationship. We were in our own world nothing mattered. Then Yes, it happened, and I got pregnant…. One time we were together, and he called home and said he needed to talk to his mom, I was in the pool, I guess he told his mother about me… He says to me my mom is on the phone she wants to speak with you!!! I was so scared I got out of the pool; she says hello…laughing why you don't want to talk with me are you pregnant? If you could have seen the expression on my face. I said yes Ma'am she said that's all right, But I look forward to meeting you real soon ok! I passed the phone back to him and he was laughing and saying alright ma! He says my mom is heavy in the church she's an Evangelist and my dad is a Deacon laughing! Time progressed and I got to meet his parent's family etc... I was about 4 months; I was really showing… came back home and I went in for my routine monthly check up and My doctor did an ultrasound and long behold he said 2 heart beats. Twins! I was shocked but it didn't surprise me like I thought; because my mom was a twin, and their father I was told on his side had 7 sets of twins. By the 6th or 7th month we found out they were both fraternal girls.

Before they were born there was 7 grand-boys, so they were the first grand-girls on his side to be born, and I was my mom's first and only child to have twins. That was jackpot to his mother. (laughing) My doctor kept telling me that I was going to have them early. they were born a month early and I had them February 14, 1991. God gave me (us) two beautiful girls. I didn't give them the rhyming names like most people because I am very different; I see them as two separate individuals and have different personalities as well as identities. People always look at twins as the same whether they are identical or fraternal. There were times I would dress them in same outfits but different colors. I left that to the grandparents I didn't want to take that away from them of everything the same. We now have a family, there were times by him being in the military; it was very hard. Being in love now, a mom, and then.... he got sent off to school in Charleston South Carolina and I lived in another city, but we made it happen, we allowed nothing to come in between us.

It's something when both are so in love. He would come home on leave all the time to see us and made sure his babies and I were taken care of but when he really needed to come home he couldn't because he used up all of his leave time and they wouldn't Grant it to him because we were not married to be considered an emergency leave but we managed to balance our lives.

Finally, when he got home his parents came and got us and took us back to his hometown to meet the rest of his family. It was so many of them, He got me away from the crowd, he could tell it was a little overwhelming for me and crowds. I really needed a breather. He took me outside, asking me if I was ok? And then, he proposed to me on his parent's porch. Honestly, I was truly shocked, we talked about being together but never talked about marriage Or. I guess I missed that one, I never expected him to ask me honestly just because we had the girls. (They say men know before we do when they are ready to marry.)

He had already told my family… I had no clue, so when I came back home, they already knew and saw the ring on my finger.

We planned for a wedding with him in school, Things were so beautiful. We both agreed not big but no more than three or four of his friends and mines for the wedding party and our colors were from his dress blue uniform. He said everything else didn't matter to him. We went back home that Sunday and he reported back to base for that Monday morning and back to a lot of tears, missing us and one another, writing and calling until he was able to come back home or for the wedding. By the time school was over and total planning for the wedding the girls were now a year and a half, when you're in love and in it, it seems so long but it really wasn't the time really started going by fast. I was busy with the girls, collaborating with the ladies in the wedding party getting pattern styles for the dresses his mother is a seamstress and not everyone lived in the same city. I was so busy and before I knew it, he was home on leave, I was a mother of two, but now getting ready from… a mother to fiancée', and bride…to a wife, a new name with the title Mrs... This was the one thing I knew for sure who and what I wanted in my life; for the rest of my life. You may be saying… you should, you're getting married! There are many people I knew and know even today that they married for other reasons not here to judge just saying. I knew with no hesitation or doubt…. No break ups or threats I'm not marrying you vice versa. Our big day is now here.

The Big Day

I was so nervous I remember waking up that morning and my shoulders were so tight that they wouldn't come down… Everyone would say why are you shrugging your shoulders I would say I'm not! I woke up like this Crying!! They took me to my appointment to get my hair done thinking that it would relax me… NO! They picked me back up, took me to get ready massaging my shoulders feeling and looking like bricks…. Nothing! If you have been down this road before of getting married and you want everything to be perfect and it seems like everything is going not the way you've expected that was me…My shoulders looking crazy, the day of. my mom relaxed (permed) my niece's hair for the first time without my sister's knowledge and her hair fell out, mind you she is my flower girl. Now at the last minute trying to figure out what to do with her hair. My sister was pissed off, she was my Matron of Honor, I found out two of the groom's men; leave dates got messed up, our wedding day was the Second of May. Their started leave day was on the Third. (Military Wording was wrong) Finally getting backups replacing people and adding people. Now all the kinks fell into place, so I thought. then we were all at the church. Ready, Set, Action.

My niece decides she's too scared and now time for her and the rose petals to come down the Aisle, my brother was coaching her.... Come on You can do It, Do it for me!! She said NO!!!!! I now am coaching her please do it for Aunt Glenda I need you!! You look so pretty I really need your help and gave her a kiss. Finally, my baby Angelica did it... My sister's boyfriend at the time had to help her walk a little bit down the Aisle. Uhh! He was one of the replacements of another groomsmen, since he was in the USMC, well it all fell into place. Now everyone was where they needed and should be; all the bridesmaids, matron of honor and groom's-men aligned up, women looking beautiful and men sharp in their dress blues... on the outside no one knew the inside kinks! (laughing) Now my turn...Lord all these folks looking at me and my brother dressed in his USCG fatigue's escorting me to my husband to be... about to be in tears for some reason I'm waving and smiling going down the aisle like I was in a Miss America Pageant and then I saw him, my shoulders relaxed and fell down I was ready for my new life. He looked at me I saw him exhale, blow and smiled at me but looking kind of nervous, I must say he was looking fine in his dress blues and me in my white gown, surrounded by his home church with family and friends.

Nothing else mattered, truthfully, I would've married him in a T- shirt and cut off shorts. This is The Man I wanted for the rest of my life.

Life was beginning

I loved him and he loved me...both in love! As time progressed, we had another child in 1993 a son. On the inside I wanted more, things were great and had a beautiful family, but something was still missing. I was invited to church, from my best friend Vanessa, along with two other friends Margret and Dave these two as a married couple was something! They would fight like cats and dogs cuss each other out; but would go to church in a minute. At the time we were all military wives. So, I visited S.P. Holiness Church where we lived in Jacksonville, NC I enjoyed myself. During service they had two lines one was for prayer and the other was for salvation. I went on the line for prayer to pray for my dad. The lady asked me what was I in need of? I said...can you pray for my dad? .... But something happened immediately! You may not believe me. like the old mothers would say....
Something got a hold of me and would not let me go! God took over my tongue and I said....
I WANNA BE SAVED! she politely moved me over to the other line LOL. I went before the church Rom 10:9 Then they had me to undress and I put on this white robe and they baptized

me right then. Now that I think of the timing, they did things right then and their; no waiting for an appointment; some churches now to get baptized it must be a certain amount of people to use the pool. I guess to conserve water or something! Or they assume you've been baptized, and they pray and send you back to your seat. Right then... I confessed out of my mouth that I am saved Instantly!!!! I heard the music playing and saw the people hollering and dancing. saying hallelujah over and over like a party. but a different kind of party. Now I'm saved! Honestly at the time still not knowing the depth of this new life called salvation. but I was excited! I remember one of the Deacons after church shaking my hand introducing himself his name was Deacon Friend. He said Child as you were in the water, I literally saw the angels rejoicing and you have a great calling and work to do for God. A great work!! Your very different.... stay with God! Yes sir! I Didn't know what in the world he was talking about I just smiled like always, but I felt great. Time to go home, I get there. I said baby I have something to tell you... he said how was church? I said great! I have something to tell you! What? I gave my life to Christ! He said what you go and do that for? See his dad was a Deacon and mom an Evangelist, sisters in the choir. So, he knew about CHURCH!! That wasn't the response I thought he was going to give...

My life Changed

My husband got out the USMC and they sent us to his hometown Fayetteville, NC. I always heard of it never been their but never desired to move their either. When we moved, we stayed with his parents for a little while. Now a different environment and attending a new church the church he grew up in when he was younger where we got married but also, now grown and never attended. I then became a faithful member at BW Pentecostal Holiness church. We finally moved into a trailer... things were great at least I thought. We lived their almost 2 yrs. and then all hell broke loose. I was diagnosed with Guillain Barre' Syndrome a neurological disease. I got it taking a tetanus shot, in other words like an allergic to vaccine shot. I was never aware of. The only reason I took the shot in the first place I was starting a new job at a daycare for our local hospital and they looked at my immunization card and said it was required every 15 yrs. so I took the shot free of cost at the hospital... everything has a price! about the second or third day after taking the shot. I started feeling weird...fingers and toes began to tingle, my tongue was numb, taste was gone BBQ ribs wasn't ribs! everything was changing and changing quickly in my body. That weekend my youngest sister came down from Virginia. She stopped to my place for a few hours before going to Jacksonville, NC. We talked for some time.... I was not feeling well. I was sitting on the couch and I got up to use the bathroom. I get in the bathroom and it became the most difficult thing to me, All I had to do honestly was pee! I sat down to pee and things were changing... My thought processes. As I type now tears running down my face because just to know the process I went through in my body; nevertheless, what my family encountered as well. (I need a moment) I finally went and now processing what to do while in the bathroom. My brain said to do but my body had to catch up. The things the average takes for granted. All of this going on just to go to the bathroom, I literally had to talk to myself ... (In detail) pee, then wipe, pull up panties, pull up your clothes, flush, turn on water, soap, wash hands, hand towel, turn off water, dry hands, put towel back, open door! (tears) I slowly walked back to the couch my legs were giving out, my sister said you ok? just lightly nodding my head, I went to sit back, and I said ...I can't breathe!!!!

I remember gasping for air.... blacking in and out. she called 911 then mom (Mother-in-law) came, I do remember mom getting me in her car. I guess 9 1 1 took too long. I also heard mom praying and rebuking the devil and saying you will not die, you will live!

no recollection. I was out again.... Last thing I remember was doctors saying Get her out of here there is nothing we can do for her send her to Duke! When I woke up tubes in my nose, I was hooked up to an I V tubes in my nose to breathe and doctors with white coats all around me. Scared, and crying. My immediate family not even my own mother wasn't even here.

   The doctor came in. Hi, I'm doctor so and so; you are at Duke Medical Hospital can you tell me what is your name? Who's the President of the United States? They were asking me all these questions for brain activity. Then they sent me for MRI, then CAT scan, and the worse of all a Spinal Tap, all I could do was cry it hurt so bad and then I was told not to move because they take the fluid from your spine... Jesus!

They finally took me to my room and around the clock doctors with white coats in and out all night and all day. I missed my kids I just wanted to go home and be with my kids.

Later that day doctors still in and out. I asked if I could eat because it's now been two days...One went to find out and came back and said no because they were afraid that my esophagus would close. Then another nurse comes back with this instrument that looked like to me a clear plastic toilet tissue rolls and I must blow into every hour to open my lungs. My legs were weak, and I could still feel this weird feeling. (You know when your arm or hand falls asleep and it feels like pins that weird feeling) Well imagine your hands and feet feeling like this all the time and never going away. Another doctor comes in checks my eyes because there were times when I tried to close my eyes and couldn't.

I literally had to take my hand especially my right eye to close it so I could go to sleep, and then check my feet for sensation. I tell you this was something. The next day I asked if I could go to the bathroom on my own and not a bedpan because it is uncomfortable and I didn't like it, the nurse helped me and I did pretty good and washed my hands I looked in the mirror for the first time in 4 days and I looked so frail and I noticed that my mouth was slightly twisted I was wondering why when I spoke it felt funny like when you go to the dentist and they numb your mouth. No one ever said anything to me! I guess not to scare me no more than how I was feeling…. A few hours later more blood work. when they left, I asked the nurse If I could take a shower it's been 4 days wiping off, and If you know me or like any other woman that was a sure enough No go for me!

Hygiene I take very seriously Lol. She agreed but with rules though…. never thought that it came with rules to shower at least for an adult. I agreed of course.

she unhooked me from monitor devices and wrapped my I V so it wouldn't get wet, then she assisted me then in I went. It felt so good to shower oh my goodness!!!

 Then suddenly, I started getting lightheaded and gasping for air…. I remembered one of her rules...she said pull the string and she will come ASAP. if I needed any kind of help. Well she came ASAP and I remember falling in her arms mind you I'm not average height for a woman I am 5'11, she ended up buzzing for help a male nurse came and I fell out on the bed sweating and just came out of the shower… they told me I fainted from the heat from the water see, Guillain Barre' Syndrome is a neurological disease….So the heat and sensations all confused… I didn't realize the temperature of the water… let's just say it didn't agree with my body nor nerves and prayerfully I didn't fall before they came. Physically and emotionally I was all messed up. Thank God for help. I woke up dressed and monitors back on.

The next day my mother-in-law and her friend Sister McDaniel came to visit. I asked for my kid's mom told me that they kept asking her where's my momma? and when is she coming back? I just cried…. Mom said she explained to them, but they were still young really didn't quite understand. They just wanted their mother. So, we all talked for a while and then said they couldn't stay long had to get back to my kids and family. As they were leaving mom went out the door first and then Sister McDaniel said as she got her purse and going out the door… Glenda You know one of the gifts God has blessed you with baby…. lay your own hands on your own self and tell God to restore you! and she left. Mind you I was still new with salvation, God, church, gifts, an all the lingo parables they talked. But I knew that I loved God and I was saved.

Previously I had been to a few house prayer meetings at Mother Davis where I got prophesied a couple of times my palms would sweat and feel like they were itching and on fire! So, they left to go home and as for me yet feeling alone…. I did mention earlier when we moved and all hell broke loose well my husband lost his job, left, moved out so I had no idea where he was. I called and he answered I asked if he would come, I was at Duke. and his response was If I come their;

there is nothing I can do for you anyway! all I could do was cry…. I was so hurt. The man I married was no longer him anymore, I now meant nothing. I found the local phone book in the drawer and picked it up; it was so heavy I looked up my Pastors number because he's from the surrounding area in Durham. I spoke to him he asked where I was? and what room was I in? again asking was I on the North, South, East, or West wing of the hospital? … I told him I didn't know… He said that he would ask for my name. He said he would come. He never did! Why? I guess he forgot or got busy! I waited and cried…. I asked God why? Why all of this? I'm 26, years old, I just got a new job to do better… It was for me, household and kids…. "You are taking care of everyone else and not yourself I'm testing your faith! I cried and cried. it was so hurtful and painful. See the process is not always easy. I must have dozed off and it was the next morning they came in for vital signs again after they left and I prayed and tears just rolled down my face and I began touching my face and legs, now my hands began to oil and I rubbed both my hands together rubbing now anointing my arms, face , again.. now with the fresh oil he placed in my hands! As I'm typing remembering as it was like yesterday. Then doctors came in asking me routine questions like my name, birthday, how do I feel, squeeze this… tapping my knees for reflex. then I asked if I could eat? We will start you with clear liquids. Jell-O (My favorite) and will see by lunch! mind you nothing in my mouth in 4 days... I didn't need liquids because I had an I V hooked to me the whole time... I was ready to eat...Lol. But very grateful for anything to go in my mouth. they monitored me.... Then light dietary light lunch and dinner was light as well. The next day a doctor came and introduced himself then a bunch of white coats came in.... 12 of them like the disciples in the Bible. He said that they were all in-training (except himself) like internship and was fascinated about me and my condition, wanted to meet me and ask me questions if that was ok with me. (I didn't find my nor this condition fascinating at all) they all took notes and asking questions... I answered their questions and then they thanked me and wished me well and left, they all had mentioned that they heard about Guillain Barre' but never met anyone with this disease, the doctor stayed I asked when was I going home? and what's goanna happen to me? he said maybe you will go home tomorrow! and as far as this disease it's not common at all; marine and soldiers had this disease-from many, many years ago and they were paralyzed or died from this We can only hope for the best honestly, I never like to tell my patients that I

don't know but this case is severely rare and
unknown for today truth is we don't know!.

It's a Journey Step by Step.........

Don't know how to feel

So, the next day I was discharged; mom came and got me. they gave me instructions and I had to follow up with my primary doctor with minimal instructions call 9 1 1 of course if having problems with breathing again, or with eating and swallowing the doctors they really didn't know what to expect either. We left I still was weak in my legs and I walked like a robot. still had to process all of this and dissect everything and every step and move, that I made. They made me a follow up appointment with Dr. Folks same day. I got their... he looked at me like as if I was a ghost. He asked me a bunch of questions and I told him that they told me to follow back up with him. He just told me to wait and they would call my name and we would do routine lab work I said ok! They finally called me he just smiled with amazement. You see when he first diagnosed me, with this he pulled out this huge medical book; that book was the biggest book I ever saw in my life.

Flipping pages, shaking his head, not sure or sure but didn't want to admit that the prognosis was bad., wanted to say what he thought but didn't want to jump the gun, nor scare me. Anyway, they did labs and we were about to leave, and the nurse called me… and said the Doctor needs to speak with you! I'm thinking Lord what else is going on in my body? He took me back to his office, we talked he said I have something to share with you… he hesitated. I said yes! my eyes watering…. I was so scared because my body had gone through so much and doctors are still playing it by ear of the outcome.

Please Tell Me What's Going On?

I must tell you that you are pregnant!!! What?! I said you may need to do this again! NO, you gave us blood and urine no need!

So, I take it that Duke Medical never told you....NO!

I can't tell you what to do but you really need to consider this pregnancy your body is weak and has gone and going through a tremendous strain, and not to mention you may have neurological damage, You've had MRI, CT, radiation etc.....and not to mention that the baby takes from you!! Talk about another punch in the face. He finished talking with me and told me to wait in the waiting area for a prescription for prenatal vitamins.

I went to the waiting area and waited... Mom said what's wrong?

why you crying? Is everything ok? What's going on?

He told me I'm pregnant…. WHAT!! YES, I'm pregnant! I told her what we talked about. So, while waiting she asked me what you going to name the baby? WHAT!!

I really wanted to say words that was not in the Bible… but I was never good with those words when I wasn't saved because they never came out right! but that's how I felt… I saw a bunch of magazines on the table and to shut her up I was in no mood. So much was going through my mind…. I could barely walk, my speech was slow, I got tired and winded very easily an I said Ebony. she laughed!!!!! Ebony That means black this time the baby may come out black he black (dark skin) your kind of dark Lord!!! and she laughed again! That was mom and her sense of humor, but nothing was funny to me. I didn't want to talk. Finally, they gave me my prescription which was prenatal vitamins and we left.

I Want to Go Home

On our way back to mom's house where my kids were, we stopped at Mother Davis house they were having noon day prayer. You could hear the people outside the door shouting and speaking in tongues and lifting the name of Jesus. We walked in and they saw me not expecting to see me and they all thought I was still in the hospital they were just praising God; rejoicing repeatedly saying Hallelujah!

There was a Prophetess her name was Prophetess Kinder, and she gave me a word from the Lord and said you're going to have another child! I remember that was my first time ever responding to any man or woman of God before saying NO I'M NOT!!

She said very politely take it up with Jesus I'm just the vessel. Remember I told you we just came from doctors no one knew but Jesus, me, doc and mom (kids' grandmother). She also said (her voice elevated) You suppose to give to the baby…. but God said the baby is going to give to you; what you need! LIFE! The Holy Spirit moved, and I fell out! (remember we are separated) What I didn't mention was like other young married couples that may go through separation you go through that breakup make up phase. Bad enough to separate but good enough too…. well you know what I'm talking about (laughing) my life was changing, I already had three small children and now another baby on the way. Well time went on…. I applied for disability…. (Denied) body still out of whack but still trusting God and going to church when I could. Every now and then I would have a dream then wake up with aroma of cigarettes…. God was telling me He's coming back. (he smoked) anyway he did return, and we tried to work things out… Eventually we moved into his grandma old house the family house and the kids liked it and they was happy. As time went on, we were really started being a family again my health was not 100% still the tingling in my hands and feet but not as bad, I could walk but still slow but slowly progressing.

Lord Have Mercy!

One Sunday morning my brother called me from Virginia. He had just got stationed there...He was always out of state in fact out of the country. (USCG) He said Hey sis! how are you? Fine! Are you sure? Yes, I am fine, and the kids are ok?! We are about to go to church, he said Ok! Are you sure you're ok? Yes!! ok sis we will talk Soon! Love you! love you too! Bye!

So, the kids and I go to church, we get home and I started to do a Sunday meal like always. My husband was gone with friends watching the game and I was expecting him to be home soon. While cooking and kids playing, I get a phone call.

Hi Glenda, you don't know me (my name is let's just say) Kay...and I am pregnant from your husband! I didn't know I had cuss words in me, and I said NO THE .... YOUR NOT! Yes, I am.... Then she began to go into details of when we lived in the trailer.... how she would be watching us, how his mom would pick me up and take me to work or grocery shopping, etc. (I didn't drive then) so I said he was messing with you then, Yes! and you saw the struggle, me sick, him no job and raising 3 kids and you laid up and got pregnant to keep him thinking he was going to get rid of me his wife! to be with you!!!! Before I knew it, I said you must be young, dumb and stupid!! I have 13 years in this marriage and 3 kids another one on the way and my kids will never Ever .... Ever go lacking for NO BODY!! mines are first! We are first! and I know my rights, I can sue you! see I'm not dumb by no means sweetie, North Carolina is a communicable state and you telling me; that you are willing and knew he was married!! I can sue you!! trust me baby you rolled up on the right one! all she could say was I know and he just passed my house walking from the store... and also said I don't want him and if I have to work 3 jobs to take care of my baby I will, I said do what you want to do and I hung up! You may be saying you had a conversation with this person for what? and it wouldn't be you! I had to go there for her sake but for me. So, when we moved in our house, she found a place not far from where we lived for them to be together….

He finally came back. (I never told him we have a conversation) he said Hey! I went in the bedroom… kids were still playing! we never did anything in front of the kids…. He came in the room we had words I broke down in tears; so, hurt and broken I was 8 months...I started cramping bad he trying to hold me I pulled away… fell on the bed. I ended up having to go to the hospital, I stayed for observation and they told me bed rest. We got back home; I was so broken. He left (I guess to get on her for telling and calling me) the kids saw me

crying and said don't Cry why you crying? where's daddy? I told them I was fine and too keep playing and have fun. Well one of them called their grandparents and said mommy is crying and daddy is gone! So, they came over and we had a conversation it wasn't good at all. Finally, he came back he wanted to explain some more. I didn't want to hear anything! Truthfully what wife does! Couple of weeks separated in the house on the couch, but under the same roof. I had to maintain for my baby and my kids. Now time to have the baby I was going to be induced but water broke same day… he came to the hospital. Three and a half hours of labor and YES, I had a girl and named her Eboni… (laughing) When man says

NO! God says Yes!! 7 lbs.9 ounces all fingers and toes as they say healthy and normal. Now 4 kids and a broken marriage I just wanted my husband and we both were still in love and wanted but now we began to get letters in the mail for child support, we never really argued about stuff now arguments about seeing this child and about coming or meeting them. No, this child did not ask to be here. No! but I didn't ask to be in this either. I didn't break our vows, and this tormented me daily... a part of his body my husband he now gave to someone else that belonged to me!! Why and How? I was so broken and hurt.... We loved each other; now.... feeling so Broken! I could not bear this longer trying, the emotions, a few years.... wanting and praying for this to go away like a bad dream. I wanted a two-parent household for my kids, for us, more than Anything I wanted my husband, what we had back, just about us and our family.... part of what I never had even as a child. My husband, my kids, house, family etc.... I called and told him that my mom and younger sister was coming down from Virginia to our house for a visit which was rare, but I was excited specially to see my sister. He was at work and said They are coming down here wow! ok! They never came to see me, that feeling again I was not good enough! My mom always compares me to my younger sister.... Always!! She has this, she has that! Why don't you this or that! and my husband would see it all the time. So, we always traveled to them. For Thanksgiving holidays or on occasions. Anyway we all were enjoying ourselves laughing and joking and I mentioned a photograph about a man in one of my mom's old photo albums and suddenly it was like a needle going across an old 33 or 45 record/album, My mom got so mad and defensive the atmosphere changed and she began cursing me out in my own kitchen...

My sister said why are you so mad and angry?! Then my mom tells us this story and then tells me about my real father...... I'm in tears and some things began to make sense and somethings I wanted to cuss (I didn't) no need wouldn't change anything. Though my husband and I had gone through so much together and individually; one thing I can say is when it was time for me to meet my extended family through the midst of our major problems he was very supportive he knew and saw how I was treated by my mom and how she handled every one of us. We always would talk and he knew a lot of my struggles I had encountered and was so grateful because this was the man I fell in love with that loved me but the wedge was there I tell you it was so painful and hurtful for the both of us. Finally, we did move out, and then later divorced. This was the hardest thing ever in my entire life. After years of hurt on both parts and finally a meaningful conversation between the both of us we never had after years of no closure took place, see for those who knew or know us there was always a love, bond, and chemistry between us even after both of us moving on...we will always love one another I truly believe even if we didn't share children; that love ...it's something else.

Deceived

After I divorced and in so much hurt and pain but wanting to move on and be happy and not hurt like this

I wanted that love I once had...So I thought. realizing and embracing the fact that I never gave myself time to heal. I was so open again not realizing many things till afterwards or being in it. There is a scripture in the Bible when it says seemingly to be right unto a man; but the end thereof are the ways of death. (Prov 14:12)

Well I ran into a brick wall. I met someone remarried and thought I was in love and received a false sense of security, ministry that I wanted, needed and longed for; for me and my kids. Despite all the hell I went through I still thank God! This marriage was a sure enough trial and test and the enemy meant for keeps! My husband started off like in some marriages nice, flattering, attentive, giving in the church, gifted etc. Later, I began to find out things, no not the average stuff like leaving the toilet seat up, clothes on the floor, toothpaste cap not closed etc.

We relocated to Colorado for a new start in our marriage and my kids to learn outside of North

Carolina and to make more money. They began to adapt, and I began to learn somethings let's just say I'm from the city! many things I've heard of or been exposed too but never ever done such things! Not passing judgement on anyone because we all have our own cross to bear.

I found out he was doing drugs! No not weed (never done that either) crack! no hearsay or speculating! I knew for myself. Came home high as a kite with shakes or needing a fix! Here I go! A brick wall....

Mind you Colorado was not a drive around the corner nor a drive to one of our local surrounding cities like when we lived in North Carolina. The kids and I had a talk and they were ready to come back home like myself, but not that easy, I was working they was in school and bills to keep what we had. I continued to work save what little left over I had and prayed.

One day I was outside trying to exhale, I remember looking around me and praying, I could see the mountains they were so pretty and looked so closely but from what I heard it took about 3 or 4 hours to get to the actual mountains. I remember the Lord speaking to me and said Glenda where does the mountains begin? and where do they end? I'm Alpha/ Omega the beginning and the end!

The Lord began to break certain scenarios down to me; When minimum wage was $4.25, I took care of you! I will always take care of you!! crying.... I said yes God. A couple of weeks later I was at work and I spoke to my boss Ms. Amanda she was so nice; she took me to her office, and we talked. I told her that I needed to go back to North Carolina things were not going well for me and my kids. She said that she hated that I had to leave because she loved my work performance, then she asked me if there was anything that she could do to get me to stay, I just said things are bad and she said I understand. So, I left out of the office, As I was heading back to my classroom, she called me back to her and said I will mail you your check can you write down the forwarding address? I said ok! I was going to use moms (kids grandparents address) Then she said no Glenda I will write out the check and give it to you at the end of the day no need to have you to wait.... I said thank you Ms. Amanda she said No thank-you! (she was smiling but you could see concern) (God I thank you....provision) The kids and I were preparing but there are a couple of things I have not mentioned with the full details of whole Colorado experience maybe in another Journey book who's to say!

It was the weekend. We piled up what we could, and we left… Left him there. We get back my kids was so excited to be back and so was I. We drove 28 hours We stayed with a friend not quite 2 months. in those two months I was working and saving for a place, he also contacted me….

yes, I took him back.

Have you ever been in a second marriage in your heart you want it to work! why? it's your second! it's almost like you are trying to prove to yourself everything you went through your first is going to be better and the flip side proving to others your happier than ever and your Good!!! Things were ok for a while then things started missing little odds and ends then my kids Nintendo their dad brought them…. I'd ask... Someone stole it! As soon as I replace things it would be gone again. Things started getting bad where I had to return furniture (bed suite) I could no longer pay for trying to replace other things.

When you think it won't happen to you?

One day I was cleaning, doing laundry and playing my gospel music like usual and I found this object in the laundry room, the laundry room was on the outside of the house. I heard but never saw nor held this object in my own personal hand before; it was a piece of burnt glass and smelled weird. I confronted him about it and for the first time ever in my life in a heated bad discussion he pushed me and pulling my hair,(at the time I had micro braids) I'm crying and swinging let my hair go… let me go! he finally let go and some of by braids were on the floor and a bald spot in my head. (I locked myself in the room crying then my youngest came in from outside knocked on the door trying to get it together wiping tears so she would not see me crying. I let her in, and she said what happened to the living-room and why some of your braids are on the floor? why you crying? He started banging on the door yelling cursing, now my baby hearing this foolishness! she started crying I want my daddy! OH BOY!!! Call my daddy!! I want to talk to my daddy! she gets the phone crying Daddy; mommy is crying…. I remember crying Jesus, then calling my baby brothers name. Then he is yelling and cussing open this mother so and so door!! you can call his name all you want! then saying if I was to call him, he was going to hurt him. He's from Durham North Carolina and knew a lot of people and they have a-lot of gangs up there.

My daughter told me daddy wants to speak with you! I did .... now he is fussing but the kind of fussing was concerned about her and me! He kept saying I'm going to get him!!

 I'm crying... he never came I guess not to get himself in trouble. He sent the police to my house! The police asked questions I asked for them to take him.... sad thing was because he had been in trouble before I thought for sure they would take him, NO! they asked me to leave!! Officer said Is that your Vehicle. Yes! in my name only! and this place is in me and my kids name! The officer says: Ma'am since you have the car, you're going to have to find a place to go!! ME? YES! to protect him and others! I said to the officer I, I have never been in trouble before, I have a clean record, I'm a citizen, I pay taxes, I never even had a speeding ticket before, I vote, and I have to leave!! Are you serious? Sorry but Yes Ma'am!

 I got some stuff Ma'am you just can't throw him out either the laws have changed. I then left... stayed at a friend. I lost so many friends and a baby brother up to this day that doesn't speak to me because of his bad behavior.... Of many things I was not aware of.

Yes, a few years of staying my thinking perception of the church, second failed marriage, and he's my husband and a soul not thinking of the effects of me and the example to my kids they have never experienced before because their father never put his hands on me in the 14 yrs. we were together married.

We moved a few times I was all over the place now that I look back. Trying so hard pushing for my kids, trying to keep my sanity and trying to do the Christian and Godly right thing! And most hang in there!

There are some other events that took place that I am not proud of but nuggets that I pray that will be able to help someone else.

Bumpy but beneficial ride!

We moved to Savannah Ga. We lived in
Pooler beautiful city, rented a privately-owned
house owner was nice and house had what I
always wanted…. a deck! I used my tax money
loaded up and off we went; new atmosphere,
new change, environment, got blessed with a
job, everything caught up falling in place,
payed one month's rent in advance just in case
we didn't land a job. Decorating house with
what I had and buying things I desired (Flat
screen) replacing desktop to flat screen for my
computer because I finally wanted to go back
to school but for business administration.
Making Changes for myself. Started decorating
my deck and had my favorite two tall palm
trees from Walmart. I even brought school
clothes and supplies to prepare for kids this
time it was for my youngest and my stepson.
my other 3 were now grown and graduated
high school and one in college. We would go

out downtown Bay street ride the ferry, go to Tybee Island land beach which was about 20 min drive. Enjoying ourselves and life.

He started his job first then I was about 2 weeks later. I would take him we still only had one car and from prior experience you're not getting nor taking my car anywhere! anyway, all seemed to be going well. I would talk to my oldest sister like usual filling her in with the move and job pictures of the house etc. Thursday morning, I got up went in the bathroom for quietness and logged in on for a prayer conference call with one of my former Apostle. We all muted the call. He began to pray, now in tongues and then gave a prophetic word. Mind you he knows nothing haven't spoken in years; many people log on from everywhere. He gave a prophetic word, but he said he didn't know who it was for.... and it hit my spirit and aligned up with the unknown he never knew about, but the Father knows everything! The call was finished, and I began to pray and cry out but low cry out not to awake him. I went back to bed before it was time for him to get up, remember I must drop him off.

I hadn't said anything as far as me leaving to go away because of my car. He would be already planning to do dirt with my car! I didn't know what to do with my car. Well when he got up got dressed then his boss called to tell him no work for the day because of the rain. He used to cut down trees, so he comes in the room happy... It's raining they pay us for half the day because of the rain so I get to stay home with you all day long!! I said all day!? Wow! (I was not happy) didn't show it.

Thinking on Friday I was to leave because I had a women's conference to attend to in Louisville, Kentucky, I was to meet my oldest sister they're over the weekend. So, I said ok! Mind you it was pouring down outside like a mini storm.

I go to the kitchen to make me some coffee in my new Keurig I just got from my sister as a housewarming gift. No more coffee pot (Laughing) I make my coffee and head back to the room, I sat down to watch TV they had two new shows out, I didn't get to see because we didn't have cable in North Carolina so I was trying to catch up on Housewives of Atlanta (Nene) and the Haves and Have-Nots. Out of nowhere; because he been stop asking me!

He says: Baby where's the keys?

Me: what keys?

Me: your house keys?

Him: The car keys? I'm going to donate (blood)

I say: It's pouring down and there's no gas in the car. which was truthful.

I said: No!

Him: NO! I'm your husband and can't even drive your car? I'm a grown A…. man, and got to ask permission to drive my wife's car?

F this…. Then he leaves out of the room…. Comes back.

Him: Then you take me!

 Me: There's no gas in the car!

Him: when I donate, I will put half in the car and keep the other half.

Me: You always say that you will put it in but it will be just enough to get you where you need to go… you don't never put it in there for us! this is about you! it's always about you! you said your home then be home! and it's pouring down outside. Do you see how bad it's raining!!!

So, I get up to get more coffee and he shoves me like back in the day in New York City when two guys would start a fight, they would go around and round saying, what you going to do? Man! what you gone do? and rub hitting shoulder to shoulder that was a way to Agitate the fight to get it started.

Well I remember those school yard fist fights that was a flash back for me.

So, I said don't shove me saying his name he said those very words back in the day. what you gone do???

I said stop!! he was laughing…. (I'm not) then he started pointing his finger in my face., I said: Get your hands out my face stop playing it's not funny!

Him: Ain't nobody laughing then he mushed me in the face. Saying….Punk!

so, I stumbled back a little. we both were in the doorway remember I was going out for coffee he was in the doorway, (crossing my path) he pushed me I said stop as I turned around….(sorry I need a moment tears because this was like yesterday to me and healing through God with this)

I turned around and he punched me in my face. I screamed so loud and crying, holding my face.

I charged with little strength I had because it hurt so bad. (His son was in the room next to our room, but he never came out to see what happened or if I was ok; he was in the 10th grade older than my daughter she was in the 9th grade. Her room was on the other side of the house and she heard me. My daughter came charging in after she heard me screaming and I heard her saying Hell No not my momma and hitting on him, we both hitting and swinging! he's on the floor saying so yawl gonna jump me!! it's like that!!

He gets up! He threatens my daughter and says I got something for you! she says good! cause my daddy   got something for you! an A_ _ whopping for you, you want some! Try me! So, we waited, got somethings packed a bag and we left headed for North Carolina.,

My daughter stayed with her twin sister for the weekend and my sister switched my ticket and I flew from Fayetteville to Kentucky. I was in pain on the flight. my face and my nose were hurting, I got their late I missed my flight, head hurting, and I was all messed up… I got they're in time to hear the last speaker and her topic was about Surgery!

How that hit home… spiritually God orchestrates and naturally how we prepare to go in… I will never forget that moment.

They had this segment where the women shared what they had learned from different speakers… I had only heard one I don't talk much and certainly don't volunteer but the Holy Ghost had his way and I began to share what I got out of what I heard and learned. I could feel God's presence resting in my lap…. It was predestined timing for me to be late... flight and all... Yes, I would have heard all the wonderful speakers. But the words he needed for me to hear as well as to say to others... There was a young lady there stood out a couple of them in the spirit began to stand out to me. As I was sharing about the healing process after surgery even from pass experience God did a shift where I began to now expound on my own personal experience that just happened to me not even 24 hrs. (I'm very private Even writing and sharing my stories for this book are not easy but God said that it's time the people need to hear) The words came out of my mouth. My husband punched me in the face.... (Topic Surgery) In the surgery process then comes healing... I needed healing just like another woman their... As I said it this young lady looked at another lady and folded her arms like... I wish someone would punch me in the face!

Holy Ghost boldness took over I walked towards her; looked her in the face....

How dare you!!!!! Don't act like you're too good or as if it ain't happen to you! You just never told it!!!!!! tears began to roll down her face and she cried. I bless God for sharing and being in position...a willing vessel.... See many times we judge others and look at others as if things never happened to you or something Is wrong with them for encountering certain things in their lives. But forget what you have gone through or too embarrassed to admit it once was you and now God must humble you. We don't know what we are going to encounter in our life.

Self- Examination Notes ....

*Pray, Acknowledge, Enjoy, and
Embrace the Journey Steps..........*

Notes. ......

The Good, Bad, and the in different ....

Got to Go Back!

I headed back got my daughter and we go back, and I tell you my house was wiped out......(Tears) (need a breather)

All my stuff was gone...You name it, it was gone even the tissue in the bathroom. All the years of hard work I already had and New stuff too. THE DEVIL...Kill Steal and Destroy. I spoke to the landlord he said he knew something was wrong because he saw a big yard sale and he had picked up rent the prior month before and came in wrote the receipt and saw me decorating and said it looked nice. I decided to clean up the place he trashed and breaking the lease so no deposit.... there went thousands of dollars for whole household furnishing and $800 deposit.

We headed back to North Carolina and my oldest daughter was in labor with my third grandchild. We were on the highway, which was a four-hour drive, while we were driving she called me on my cell, Momma hurry!! I told her we have two hours to go before I get there, finally get to hospital washed my hands said hello and not even 10 min.... Push! My granddaughter was here! she waited for me(lol) I cut the cord and we left, went to my friend's house crashed about 3 days and God blessed and I got an apartment. they paid the first 3 months I was out looking for a job all doors closed… it was never hard to find a job especially in my field. Daycare! but it was. Daily I kept getting headaches I was used to migraines because I use to always get them as a child. I never knew what a headache was…… Until one day as I was driving my daughter to school, we were praying in the car like usual but extra because they had 10th grade mid-term exams. I prayed with her… we was at the light and I closed my eyes for a few seconds cause my head was hurting waiting for the light to turn green and as I opened my eyes I saw black spots...I shook my head to clear my vision … it did for a while I didn't say anything to my daughter, she just thought I was tired because she knew I had a hard time sleeping at night. I dropped her off and told her to have a blessed day! I'm heading back to apartment...forgot my tablet most mornings I would go to Starbucks to use Wi-Fi, to look for a job and use my gift cards my sister gave me when her and my brother in- law came from Ny to buy me some clothes because I now didn't have any… Gone! As I was driving, I heard the Lord say Go Now! Go to the Hospital…. I went and long behold they said to me I don't know how you did it this long …. the x-ray shows you've been walking around with a concussion...They asked me a bunch of questions they talked to a social worker and domestic violence counselor. They all were nice but now crying and Embarrassed! A woman of God! and Domestic violence.... I answered everything truthfully and honestly. They discharged me I had two prescriptions to fill and made me sleepy. I followed the doctor's instructions not to sleep too long due to a concussion, so that was scary. So, I had her sister to pick her up from school so I could sleep. She asked but I told her I went to doctors and they gave me medicine that made me sleepy and I couldn't drive which was truthful.

Daily I would search for a job and no door would open. Finally, I had to put our things back in storage. My daughter stayed. I ended up going back to Savannah. I got my old job back with no problem, I thank God for favor, but I knew I had to face somethings unfinished. See when you are a child of God somethings you still must handle in a certain manner and do it his way regardless how someone else has treated or mistreated you! When I did it one way... God would turn around and say what did you say? What did you do? Uhh It was like restarting over like re-taking a test all over again... Linking back was hard for me especially when you have anger, rage, and thinking if you can really get away with things like, baking a cherry pie (his favorite) with a little something in it. It seemed like it was reality like a movie and watching tv show Snap. This was not me and certainly not of God!

I would never hurt anyone. I snapped out that crazy stinking- thinking quick! (PRAYER)

I love orange but not 24/7 or for life for nobody and I'm locked down while he's running around free and I have kids, grandkids and a life to enjoy No ham! No ma'am! No turkey sandwich!

I love my freedom. I tell my friends…. everyone has their own ministry and own lane; but jail house is not for me.

Yes, Lord Hallelujah!!!

Every day I prayed and shared somethings with God because God knew I was on the edge.

One day an opportunity presented itself and I took it. I said to him I'm going back home I did what I was supposed to, and I have a daughter that I am responsible for... I'm a mother first!! So, I got all my little belongings and got in my car and hear he comes saying I'm going! are you? I'm not coming back to Savannah! He says That's fine! I need to take care of something there anyway! So, I'm on the phone with my prior landlord I had rental history with for years. We spoke he said he had two available properties and I could meet with him later that day about noon. So, he hears conversation then says that's good! We get to North Carolina. I went to see my kids and I crashed with my kids till I met with landlord.

He was somewhere. He came by my daughter's house because he knew I had an appointment. Ok God here we go! He went with me to both places trust me I didn't want him to know anything...But God! I chose a place and I sign then he said I'll sign too! I was about to lose it... God said peace! I said nothing.... he signs; I gave him first month rent and he worked with me with the deposit.

Landlord leaves he smiles we did it! WE … I go upstairs and he said I'll be right back! (uhm great!!) I get my daughter and show her around after going through what we did I never wanted her to go through pain… (She hated him and had every right) We cleaned up, wiping things down and he came back. I took my daughter back to her sisters. We went and got my little bit of stuff out of storage I did have that I had left here from before. and headed back to the house. He slept in another bedroom. My daughter was in my room every day. This was all crazy to me, but God said peace! A week went by now it's Thanksgiving Day I cooked the kids and grands came over. he was there for a few minutes then left. (my kids did not want him there and he knew it.) He never ate but came back with a plate from a church. Everyone left and me and my daughter went upstairs to lay-down for a nap. We woke up he was gone. So, my daughter and I spent time together watching a movie and eating pie, then we played a two-man game on my tablet, it died so we put on the charger and went to bed. The next morning, we woke up and I'm looking for the tablet to play music and it was gone. So, I asked my daughter does she have it she said no! you had it on the charger last night! My gut said here we go!!! I was right it was gone the last little thing I owned as far as electronics… I waited for him to come back from wherever he was...while waiting I'm praying, mad, and crying to God I had Enough!!!!

Hours later her returned like nothing was wrong.... I called him by his name... where's my tablet? what are you talking about!! I don't know! Girl .... it's probably where you left it!

(it's his game) I said I left it on the charger, and it's gone. Here it is...

you crazy! I took the tablet in the room my daughter was in there; we both sat on the bed and went to plug it in to charge it and the port where you charge it was damaged as if someone took a knife to try to pry it open.... Are you serious! Damaged!

I called him and I tell you I felt this feeling I never felt before EVER.... God gave me the words with boldness and authority this was HIM! POWER!!

To call out the different words and spirits in the atmosphere that he carried.... The Devil.

God even gave me a word for myself of how it was a plan for the enemy to take me out! he even gave me specific scriptures of the plan from the enemy!! So, as I called the spirits he backed up!!! and started going downstairs. As he went downstairs, I was still rebuking, and I told him what was led for me to say and then said GO!!!!!!! Just like you and the enemy had a plan God had and has a plan for me... You set yourself up! Legally Biblically as well as with the Law of the land. God said no more as of today this day!!!!!!! Don't come back, don't leave anything behind to try to come back to get it. Here's your things and the rest I will sit to the curb. God says Done!! Get the HELL out!! Now you are cussing me out! (I can't offer you HELL) I told God I never want to see him ever again. After that, there were times I knew he came around the house I could feel this eerie feeling... sometimes I was even fearful to sleep, mind you there were times I hardly slept because I would think about my car keys being gone in the middle of the night and no car to go to work or things missing from the house. Some may not understand and ask why did you put up with all of that? or why so long? I have answers to most of these questions. I truly thought this was it! the one...Things fell in place in the beginning and seemed to be right...talk, facade to be something he was not. church, musician, ordained minister and wanted in so many ways, the fight I wish I had to fight for my children's father my love but how...? I know I'm not the only woman who thought like the bible says seemingly to be right but wrong. I wanted love, to be in love again and I wanted my marriage to work; but not for the cost of my kids and my life. When you marry for the second time you truly want it to work and even more than your first like you are really trying to prove to yourself, others and to save the embarrassment that it failed again.

I thank God that through it all I stayed with God and pushed to be the woman I am today...I can effectively minister to others on the things I have encountered. I have been emotionally and physically abused and can say that to another woman now. I have been abused more emotionally than physically and no woman wants to openly admit that a man... especially your husband has done that to them. I had to mentally get to a place where I knew I was hiding. I would smile and laugh but the pain inside and still had to minister to others on different levels. The blessing was God cared but didn't care about all that…. I still had to push through the tears and all… Days when I said God, I don't want to do this anymore! And then someone would call me ...Evangelist Glenda can you pray for me now! (God's sense of humor (Really)

 Here I go PRAYING! Or at an event… there I go, through all of this; there is always a testimony…. trust me!

I have been through so much but always remembering that God is always with me, I know that he will not put more on me then I can bare. The things that I have encountered is truly for my making. No, I am not perfect by any means, so flawed but I strive every day to be a better me.

Yes, I desire one day to remarry I don't push or force, I am in a hurry but I'm not in a rush if that makes sense to you! He knows me and my heart's desire. And will send me the right one, until then I've been single some few years now being single and I'm getting to learn and know me, my who, what, when where why and how, before I say I do to any man. Marriage is ministry and work. I did have the bitter taste in my mouth for a minute. I didn't want to talk nevertheless like men do, they would look... but I put that wall up so bad like don't even look at me. But in my mind Lord I want to be married, of course for all the right reasons and commitment and companionship and all the above but how was that possible (Crazy) but realizing every man is not the same. There are some good men out there willing to except me for me. Love is beautiful and God Is Love, this is the very thing that I minister about all the time.

Ministering God's word

In the process of all of this I had to still go and minister God's word even when I didn't feel like it, and it is not easy, see sometimes he wants to see your faithfulness and will test you. Going to church, ministering and times I had to travel and go. Many times, I had to put me on the back burner of my issues because it's about you; for a hot second, enough for that light bulb to turn on and then quickly it's about God's people... A man and woman of God told me that in my ministry there is a great need. That people need me and my transparency. I am Honored and too God be the Glory! Don't get me wrong its important truthfully, when it comes to proper protocol with titles and positions. I don't care about titles or positions and numbers If I can help to reach that one person then I am good. I've traveled for one... No, I'm not a big time anything! I rather stay low and humble. I stay in my lane; every now and then God Will have me to shift lanes because; we can't always stay in the same lane. For example, when you're driving on the highway you got to move over or get out of the way. I get out of the way in the spirit as he leads for growth, But I stay in my lane, I don't pretend to be someone I'm not, I don't want to be like so and so... I am me. I love how he can have me at your house, and the atmosphere changes and here he goes!!! Or on the phone... Yes, in the pulpit but knows I'm honored but it is well if I'm not. I've learned especially from the South and church folk... it's about name, and how you whoop and holler, money and attire... Don't get me wrong I'm not bashing the church nor people but from my experiences. I've heard people say if you don't pay them this I'm not preaching!!I' I'm not crazy and I do understand it takes money to travel, pay bills and live but you said Lord send me I'll go (whoops). But because they won't pay you your worth you won't go... You complain on your natural job that they don't pay you enough to do what you do, but you still get up and go anyway!! (oops) People associate people by name who you are ... a somebody or a nobody! associate you by the church you go to and the pastor's name and according to membership numbers and it's sad... We are to go into any house to reverence our Lord and Savior and worship him in spirit and in truth. Receive Gods word, apply, live it to the best of our ability, teach others, invite and tell the good news. Allow no one to take away what God is doing in you and your relationship with him. No matter what I went through I never stopped pushing more for God. I've experienced and ministered to others where they stopped and gave up.... I love God and want to please him;

many will not understand and may say it doesn't take all of that or I'm too Holy! No, I'm not perfect by any means I love to laugh, cut up and have fun, I never think nor thought that I was better than anyone, but I have a standard for myself and I don't play when it comes to God. I experienced once when I had someone interested in me and it was mutual on my part as well calling, texting, dining ... His title/position was higher than mines a Bishop and has a church he wanted to sleep with me and because I declined that was the end of that. No phone call or discussion but a text to say I'm sorry but after praying this is not going to work for me. I texted back Thank You! I wasn't mad or anything, I prayed God said it's not you its him. Touch not my anointed and do my prophet no harm! See I had already prayed God I want what you want, and I mean business. I've been down this road call crazy and foolishness. there are times because I am an Evangelist I am not invited to certain things or I get the cliché conversations from people putting on airs when I am human and I want you to be you because I am; I have no heaven or hell to put anyone in I have to answer to God just like the next person. You can have fun and live...It took me a long time to find me and embrace my life and I am living, enjoying God and ministry and loving me even the more, Step by step enjoy your life.

Transition Time Ready or Not

There has been quite a few people to tell me they see me taking off, traveling and that my ministry is unique; one told me he even saw wings on the side of a plane with my name on it traveling and it's not just here in the US... International (wow to God be the Glory) I receive in Jesus name. He has all our plans and timing in his hands.

A Few years ago, I had to go back home to New York to support a ministry that God told me to help to establish their church. Long behold by being obedient the Lord elevated me during the service to Evangelist, and with the charge of Ambassador. The spirit was so high, we were sure enough having a Holy Ghost time; It was Easter Sunday. I remember hearing My brother in-law from the pulpit saying where is Glenda? with an urgency where's my sister in law? My God My God! now coming out of the pulpit where? where? Where is she? him saying I hear you God!

I raised my index finger and softly said here I am... I'm right here Pastor Troy. and he kept saying today! Today!!!

God says Today! Resurrection Sunday You will be licensed / ordained here! Help me Holy Ghost because I hear you loud and clear YES God Yes, I hear you! Many knew I was already doing the work as an Evangelist honestly for years and I didn't realize or thought I was doing the work and again honestly content without a piece of paper. He did all the proper protocol and others were installed as well. One thing about my brother in-law he moves when God moves, he publicly said to the church afterwards yawl don't think because this is my sister, she gets this because yawl know better!! God said! And I do what God says. Hearing some say we know Pastor. God took me all the way back home to my birthplace. I bless God to choose me, it's an honor but it's not easy and I don't take it lightly, Once the title came people really expected more from me and more pressure. Sad thing is many carry a title as well in the fivefold ministry and dare not want or allow anyone to have that type pressure on themselves, but will put it on you...We often don't see ourselves and often forget we are human, I've lost what you would say friends, acquaintances because of inconsideration of myself and the spirit of manipulation. No fault of my own but for speak up and distancing myself because those are not friends. I love doing to the work of the Lord and daily I am learning, I am a woman who loves and wants to please the father. I am not perfect, and people really need to understand ministry is not perfect nor the people we have everyday situations just like the next person and we are humanly flawed and not God.... When you are called to do a work for the Lord it's not easy nor did God say it was going to be easy. I thank him for choosing me this city Brooklyn girl who has been through hell but still in the midst of everything I still thank and praise God I still give him Glory it's all for my making, I had and have to go through some stuff to become a better me, for me and to be able to speak, minister or preach more effectively . You can't tell somebody something if you haven't been through anything! I am very transparent and must meet people right where they are. People want to hear the realness out of others that can relate, it took me some time but now I can openly share my trials and test the good the bad and the indifferent. I have been physically abused, not loved by my mom, molested, no father, I've had to live in motel, divorced, evicted, car repossessed, lost my niece and have had to fight for my life with a neurological disease. In all of this I didn't lose my faith, stop loving God nor blamed God, Somethings I put on myself and most God ordained because he gets Glory! It reminds me of the scripture (Matthew 22:14 KJV) For many are called and few are chosen. I thank him for choosing me…. We all have a work to do and I try to do my best with love and move on

(2Corinthians 4:9 KJV) Persecuted, but not forsaken; cast down, but not destroyed. He is always with me every step.

She's Gone!

The last of the family members gathered in unity, we leave the hotel and now all gassed up from the local gas station also got snacks payed for the items and-as I was walking out I saw a newspaper with Angelica's funeral I went back in line and the cashier began to talk about her and the tragedy of what happened and said she was a sweet girl so I said thank you, then she said did you know her, I said yes ma'am she was my first niece her mother and I are sister's. She said baby I am so sorry.... you can take the newspapers free of charge; I said thank you and we left. We now GPS to head out to highway but it took us to the route of passing the church where we just had the funeral. Didn't know we had to pass or go by their again.

I kid you not as soon as we were passing the church my daughter said momma take a picture of the church and I did and saying Angelica auntie loves you and I will not forget about you... My car started making this noise, so I asked my daughter is that my car. She said No!! Then what is that? That is my car then it just cut off.... no lie just cut off! and behind us was the church in the rear-view mirror. The other half of the family turned around; we were all headed back home to North Carolina together we all lived in the same town. We tried to figure out what was the problem but couldn't. I called my insurance company for roadside assistance…. They finally came and long behold you will never believe me, but they towed my car, directly across the street at this auto mechanic shop where they just buried my niece Angelica… The family gets out we speak to the mechanic then called Angelica's husband because he's from this town, The mechanic changed a belt we try to leave went up the street to a stop sign and problems again, mechanic could still see us he walks up the street to us and tries to drive it and says now I think I know what the problem is…. We talked for a bit told him my nephew was on the way, he mentioned the big funeral on yesterday and how sad it was and asked if we knew her… I said yes sir , that was my niece and that's her husband that is on his way... he says I know him and his grandmother, this is a small town… sorry for your lost so he gets there, they exchanged words, so I knew now that it was a good place and God just didn't allow for this to just happen. So, we found out what the problem was, it was my engine it gave out!

Lord have mercy...The mechanic gave us a deal, but it still was money$$ Now no car in Texas and the rest of my family had to head back due to work. So, they piled up in my daughter's vehicle and their grandparent's vehicle and headed back. My Auntie called back the hotel we all were staying at and got me a room and they gave her a discount on the room again... I got my things and took it to my room. It was like I could feel her saying don't go!

I did a lot of praying and crying a couple of times my Aunt called to check on me and suggested for me to go get in the jacuzzi to relax. I did but that feeling and now your alone not around anyone. The mechanics called me and said they had to order the engine and it would be about three days. I couldn't get mad nor complain no need plus; what I could do... Can't change anything! I was still so heartbroken my baby was gone, and there was nothing that I could do to fix that either, her husband called to check on me and the status of my car and If I needed anything. Then I'm extending back to him as well, he's my nephew and hurting he just lost his wife and now raising his boys without their mom they were 7 at the time. I ordered pizza and ate of it for 2 days... and that Wednesday morning I woke up showered and mechanics called to say my car was ready! I called my nephew he came and got me, and he took me to a couple of places that was on our way to get my car. I saw the school that the boys (twins) attended and Angelica worked, he showed me the side entrance door she would come out to meet her to have lunch, the track field and then also showed me where her car was impounded from the accident as well as the school bus and the tractor trailer truck that killed her... (investigation) we sat there staring it felt like the world stopped for a moment.. we both trying to hold it together. As he drove off saying I just want my wife.... my insides screaming Angelica!!!! he told me how the hospital sent him this out landaus medical bill for the air vac after the accident and her not even a week of her being gone, we get up the street and see the cemetery with all the flowers and you see a bunch of blue from her sorority sister's then told me he has to order a plot and it takes a few months before it will be on her grave, so he will continue to put flowers their until it comes in. Then we got my car, remember I told you it was across from the burial site. We paid and he got my things put them in my car and I followed him back to the hotel. we talked outside for a while we embraced then he said he was going to the boys school to eat lunch with them and then said the school wanted to honor Angelica and plant a tree, We hugged again he left and I went upstairs and got my things…. I felt in my spirit Is wasn't ready to go yet… So, I checked out, loaded my car and then…. I called my other niece Mia and headed to Houston four hours away! This was my first time in Houston, and it was huge like New York and freeways everywhere, cars jumping off and on different highways! Houston got it going on yawl; As for me I didn't know and had known idea about anything at this point in my life but; I knew I just wasn't ready to go back. I got to my niece's place met little Cashmere her support dog and she helped me with my things we went upstairs, she had a beautiful apartment , she showed me everything and where things were, showed me my room I would be staying in and welcomed me, we both was hurting but there for one another. I remember us talking for hours and reminiscing about Angelica and church events and life stuff, both sitting up eating snacks and then her telling me whatever I needed to let her know, what we didn't have we would go out and get, and it didn't matter how long I stayed to take my time, and even if I wanted to stay permanent that was not a problem. We went out for a bit shopping and then I said I wanted to go to Wal-Mart to get a small tablet /laptop for me to start writing…. She said writing! I said yes that I wanted to write a book, she was so happy and said that's what's up Aunt Glenda and she supports me in this. I told her me and Angelica had this conversation quite a few times and she told me that I needed too… She also agreed that the book was necessary and how my transparency would help others. So, I purchased my items, and we got some other things and we left… I began to write for the next two three days; I would come out of the room but then right back in the room trying to get all of this out of me but also condense my stories and testimonies about ME!

I am a listener so all the times when I did try to write whether on paper in a journal or typing it was very hard especially after writing and I would re-read and it would be so painful to read it and then embarrassed because what's in your head no one knows about but on paper is a whole different ball game. learning that I had to embrace it and that I was not the first nor the last to encounter the things I went through or going through, but the message must get out there and must be told also to all others to know that no one is perfect. I won't lie this is not easy at all, but I had to face it just like in the mirror; Yes bad things do happen to good people and like the bible says something good is coming out of this and it did I have full mobility of my body, only through the grace of God. I beat all the odds of what the doctors said o I would be paralyzed for life or die. No, I can never take a flu or tetanus shot. (that's ok!)

or it will kill me. My last child is healthy and normal for what we perceive normal to be. All my beautiful kids graduated High School, and some chose to go to College, all living productive lives, praise God. I am so grateful for life. I'm a grandmother (Nana) of now 5. There was a time when I would stretch myself so thin and a walking time bomb. Meaning things in my personal life, then work, bills, so called friends pulling on me only to benefit themselves. Today would never admit! So, I separated, and God did and is doing the rest. People would PREY on my kindness for weakness for years. Then I began to start praying differently God I mean it from my heart and everything within me even if it hurts I don't care if I met them 5 minutes ago or 45 years ago, remove people that are not beneficial for my life, that are poisonous , and toxic to me, allow no attachment, I don't care who they are friends, family, colleagues, relationships and especially people in the ministry…. manipulative!!

People are something else they expect from you but won't put in the work for themselves and dare for you to challenge them… or you let them go, now you're the problem and now you're the one acting funny. So, I've learned to free them and free myself. If you don't, I'm telling you from experience you will be the one up all-night praying, and crying to God, while they are in the bed resting and not thinking about you or what they said or done to you! Give it and them to God and find peace within yourself and start to live again for yourself with happiness. I've experienced so much in this long/short period in my life, mostly trying to fit in… trying to find my place with people and acceptance at one period of time in anyone's life if you can be truthful and embrace that moment …we all wanted to fit in and feel excepted. Again, when your told early on or heard someone or people say certain things; that's internal so now you carry stuff… I had to let go.

Through God still learning to let go. You may be asking well how did you get over this? Daily process and through Christ; Knowing that I am who he says that I am.

I am beautifully and wonderfully made. He created me the way he saw fit... to be tall, crooked teeth, but love to smile, big eyes to see, very quiet, can use my voice, shaped his way, So who am I to tell God or get mad at him because I didn't see myself the way society says I should look! That's a slap in his face because he predestined you and me and when he made you and me, he didn't make no junk! This book is not written just for women... But and for our hurt, pains and issues, let me explain something when the time comes for me to minister or how ever God sees fit to use me, I make it plain for everyone to understand and to reach everyone. There are men out there who minister, have insecurities, abandonment issues, trying to correct bad behaviors, health issues, trying to live right, have been molested and divorced and remarried as well.

Truth be told, we all have a story to tell some may feel that theirs are not meant to be shared, and some can be transparent like myself and tell, it's all up to the individual. I have some things now I want to do and will write another book whether it's on a small scale or large scale with the mindset now to accomplish what I want and not what people expect of me going around in a circle and wanting and waving a flag and no one seeing me, they see only what I can do for them and how I can benefit them. So, I got off the Roller-Coaster (always hated that ride and was on it for years) Now with bravery and courage. Because mind you there are going to be someone that will read this and say is she talking about me and many will understand because they to know me and have been down some of the roads with me and some are to selfish and will discard everything enough for them to read to see did I mention their names... But here I am free in this journey, step by step through God's grace and mercy to for fill one of my dreams and accomplishments and that's too write my first book.

Through Christ I have the courage to write and share more with others

Now writing a book, writing down things and places I want to go and things I want to do and not just what falls in my lap. You know that phrase are you living? or are you just existing? Yes, I was alive don't get me wrong. I give Glory out of everything in my life, but I now see things in a different perspective. There is a big world out there I don't have the answers for everything, I don't have millions of dollars truth be told not even thousands but I have God, he knows and Sees all and has everything I need so I trust, thank and believe him at his word therefore that makes me to be rich. I know many people that have the money, house and two cars, married, and still empty… Therefore, I know he didn't bring me, nor you this far to leave me.

My Writing process began.

Two years ago I had encounter some painful hurt when my niece Angelica passed away it felt like I was ripped apart we had this amazing relationship that we both treasured Yes we all have a time for everything just as the Bible speaks in the book of Ecclesiastes the third chapter but we just don't know when, No one ever wants that wee night hour phone call to say PRAY with urgency and then an hour later the phone rings to say that the person has died (our baby died) Devastating an indescribable feeling Now gone.

 She would call me for anything! we had as she would say... I want to talk to my auntie.... that would be the Life talks! and then those talks like best/ sister/ friend talks! she would ask and we both knew the difference (laughing) It's not ironic that as I am typing the hour is approaching when I received the call from my older sister to pray that she was in a terrible car accident and fighting for her life coming from what she loved to do, from a track meet; with her students. It was all over Texas news. She passed away at the hospital at the age of

30. She had a husband and twins' boys I (we were devastated) I miss her so much, that beautiful smile and her perseverance was amazing. I remember when she was a newborn 2 days old coming from the hospital and my sister introducing me to her and her to me then handed me her and said now, I'm tired and I am going to lay down for a while. That bond never ended, When I was pregnant with my third child, she called me and said you're going to have the baby on my birthday and that's going to be my baby! really? yep! Love you aunt Glenda bye! And hung up. She was a mess! Long behold whatever she spoke happened... April 10th. I had my son, years down the road my second granddaughter is also April 10th. When we would have those memorable moments she told me I want twins like you and she did but she had twins boys!, I want to teach like you; my teaching is in the childcare field she did that too but continued and taught in Elementary School System, and track coach, track that was her thing when she first went to college.

Remembering that priceless moment when she called about the love of the life and how he asked to marry her, and she turned him down previously a couple of times wanting to finish school first. That conversation was beautiful like one of the talks I would love to have with my girls one day! Because she would listen. I said do you love him. Auntie! uhm yea! Are you in love with him? Yes.! Now does he love you? of course! Not because of the boys and the right thing to do. Listen to me…Listen to me well, she got quiet. I asked the question is he in love with you? because there is a big difference… She paused and you could hear it in her throat and started crying…. Yes, Ma'am he does! Then what's the problem? sniffling getting herself together see auntie that's why I called you! You always…. and we laughed. Later, that day she called me back; we got to pick a date I said ok! when? She said that's why I called you!! (Laughing) I said baby it's not when I pick the date, she called me back and said Sept 1, 2015 I said I will be their…. Aunt Glenda your coming all the way to Texas? Yes, ma'am I will be there. you're my first niece, you're my baby! she responded in that beautiful voice of hers I miss so much! she was never afraid to use nor Express That's my Aunt Glenda and I told her see you in a few months.

We prepared and drove to Texas it was a 13-hour drive. checked in hotel where my younger sister was and next morning was her big day! We all get dressed and went to the venue; it was so beautiful…. just like her. We go to her dressing room knocked on the door and the person says we're not letting anyone else in.

my sister said what the ….!!!!! I knocked and said it's Aunt Glenda and Aunt Teisha, we heard Angelica's voice and she said My auntie is here!! open the door...we walked in she embraced my sister and started crying when she saw me and her bridal party looking gorgeous. They all yelled NO don't cry! No tears !!!! your makeup and we all laughed, and they sat her back in her chair preparing her because everything was about to start in about 30 minutes. My baby looked so beautiful. Talk about a beautiful wedding and a beautiful day. We all miss her so much she was a beautiful person It hurts and brings tears to my eyes thinking and typing the words she was in the form of pretenses…. No longer here! but I embrace her timing here on earth and those memorable moments and hours of conversations we both shared when we talk. Today is March 31 the day we buried our baby two years ago. I'm filled but doing somethings now in my life we both discussed privately and one of those things was writing my book. She always said I needed to do this, and that people need to hear what I have to say. At times I wish that I did this sooner, She was not just my niece but supporter in so many areas, I use to tell her you always said I was always there for you but you encourage and support me in so many ways and we would laugh ….it's been years to express certain things, own and embrace the good, bad and the indifferent. So many ways I still feel her ..I remembered at the hotel after the funeral so many people and so much love she stretched out to people remembering one time when she said to me Aunt Glenda when I make it big one day you're going to make it big too! During my preparation to go to Texas for the funeral I get a phone call from Eldest daughter and she said momma some man from the radio in Texas is trying to reach you about Angelica, So I gave him your number and he said he will call you. Sure, enough a news/radio caster called me on the phone for an interview... He said that he heard about the fatal accident and someone directed him in Texas to call me! He told me that he would ask me a series of questions and then he asked for my permission to be recorded live. I asked if he could call me back an about 15 minutes or so, he agreed (I called my sister her mother out of respect and she said yes that's your baby too) He called back I agreed to do the interview, then told me he was going to asked me a series of questions and would tell me when he would start recording. He asked me if I was Aunt Glenda I said yes! In my mind honestly, I was wondering why he asked me that! anyway, then told me to share somethings about her and our bond. I got so overwhelmed that he did Express his sympathy to me and our family. The interview was easy but so hard at the same time. He thanked me for doing the interview Then asked me if I would text or email him pictures of her running track and a picture of me and her together, so I did, He received them and thanked me again. (Her way of big! and sure big for me; she knew I didn't like to talk much (laughing) TV/Radio too much! Two days later my sister calls me she was already in Texas preparing for the funeral and told me that they heard me on the local news talking about Angelica and that our pictures was in the local newspaper as well. What?!!! Wow!! my sister began to cry and then we hung up. We left that Friday all my kids, grands and even my ex-husband (children's father) and his parents. We finally get to the hotel the town she lived in was not that big so everyone knew the big story of what happened So the hotel attendants knew and so many people even a bunch of our home church members from New York was there in support mind you my sister and brother-in-law are Pastor's many, friends, family, her extended family , her co-workers from the school came.. Many I didn't know but would greet me as Aunt Glenda.... I guess Angelica would speak of me in conversations, then some would say I heard so much about you, nice to meet you! You and her look alike. I remember one of my nieces left the room and I went to the restroom I still had my shades on my eyes were so red and swollen but looked small... and as I came out the bathroom, I heard her voice saying DON'T CRY AUNTIE! STOP HIDING, YOU'RE ALWAYS HIDING! IT'S OK! LET THEM SEE YOU! No lie I was looking around no one else was in the room, I just cried Gellica...... Gellica? So, I took my shades off got myself together it was so many people I had to excuse myself and I couldn't imagine what my sister was going through. I went back downstairs down by the lobby there was a lounge that's where the hotel people had us. I couldn't wrap my mind around all of this, all these people and we didn't even have the wake or funeral yet. My baby gave so much love and was truly loved. So many amazing things took place, but the pain was and is still there, but God! At the wake the Mayor of the city came and spoke, we were so proud of her and filled with grief at the same time. The next day was the funeral and the city shut down many things in her honor, after her passing few days after everyone returned back home the school contacted my sister and told her in remembrance of Angelica they was planting a tree in her honor, and a local restaurant is honoring her as well so when you first walk in the restaurant there in her home town is a picture of her. She truly left behind a legacy. Everything she wanted she accomplished, she truly made it happen and yet so young. I truly miss my best friend and niece loved and never forgotten. I want to share something with you I was never big on dreaming what I mean by this is because I have always been a survivor, I took life as it came, I have endured somethings with being saved. Remembering my niece, we would talk and share all the time for hours and she would tell me auntie live; your kids... my cousins I grew up with are now all grown. Live and be happy. Don't be scared get married again, go back to school, you love to minister, go visit Roots! (We would laugh) One of my favorite movies. I would watch it for hours for years!) saying travel whatever makes you happy like you tell me. I go back and think about her often I can say Yes; I have done some traveling but never really thought of big-time trips big time anything and say one day and mark it off a list. I was always living for now if I go, I go.... if not no worries.... Limiting God, I believed that he can, I guess I never asked, I felt like there were more important things in my life going on than traveling just because... I would get excited for others and to them they thought that I was always gone but it was for ministry, but they wouldn't know that I would pray; I may or may not have the mean at the time. I tell God if I want to go or ok to go, pack my bags and wait on him. I would give him something to work with. As I began to grow and through ministry and life it really has enlightened me to the point I will tell you truthfully some places I've gone to that I never thought and some now I desire, and I dream of now Roots!....(tears and laughing) And I know I am going to visit those places and it won't be just a dream but a reality. There has been times I've prayed when I knew I wanted to move I would start to go get boxes and start packing daily before I knew it the whole place would be boxed up and nowhere to go, times because I wanted change and other times for my life. Lord I'm packed money is slim to none and moved in the city or out of state and literally trusted God. Some places have literally been only for a season or an assignment lesson. Remembering that our time length is not his and his season is not ours. Moving was one thing but dreaming at this age in my life it's astonishing, and beautiful. I tell you that it's never too late to dream nor write down goals... I am one of those honestly to dream I wanted a reality you know how you can just dream and dream and nothing happens... I guess that's why I didn't like to dream and never wrote anything down. I always felt stuck and things were always so hard for me and not positive; as much as I tried to make things to be positive. Because I am that believer that no matter how bad it looks someone is always worse off and the word says that all things work together for the good (Romans 8:28)

KJV) Outside of my niece before she passed pushing me to write this book and as I was writing I thought of a person that I dream to meet that behind all this writing has helped me pull somethings out of me embracing the journey steps I would love to meet not for wanting anything but a hug and humbly to say thank you! Iyanla Vanzant I would watch her shows I hate to say show because its ministry and I too am a minister of Christ; that there is no performance.... Its Ministry; But I understand because it is on TV. When writing this book, I would cry, take a break, regroup, relate many times, embrace, do the work and then I go back to writing and start all over again. I thank God for helping me take the steps because without him I could not have this. God said for me to take bigger steps. He meets me where I am on my level and I so love him and I am so grateful

NOTES.......

Remember That Everyone Is on a Journey path.

It's a Journey....... Step by Step

This book has my own personal and detailed stories that became life testimonies. I have Learned to embrace them with the good, bad and the in differences. Life is not what I always wanted or planned. I've Learned that God has his own set of plans. I was Born Glenda J Clarke Of New York City, a mother of four and a Nana of 5 thus far, I am an ordained Evangelist, love to travel and meet new people. I am an advocate for children for the past 25 years in the daycare setting. My mission is to empower others and Children as well knowing that they are loved and have a voice. I pray that this book has been inspiring and helpful to you; as well as to many others. May God continue to bless you, keep you and direct you in your journey path; step by step.

Founder of: MyJourneyYourJourney2

MyJourneyYourJourney2@yahoo.com

Made in the USA
Columbia, SC
14 November 2019